B

Praise for *Objects In Mirror Are Closer Than They Appear*

de Gutes writes with compelling honesty, and the book is a triumph of coming to terms with herself and her world.
— Claire Luchette, *Los Angeles Review of Books*

de Gutes recently won a Lambda Literary Award, beating out the likes of Cat Cora and Carrie Brownstein for this innovative, associative, autobiographical work of creative nonfiction. The book is structured as a collection of memory essays that chart the milestones in this particular lesbian's life, gradually piecing together the demise of her 23-year marriage. It's a bittersweet book, with recognizable references to Ikea furniture, cherished shared possessions, and the keepsakes that trace a meaningful relationship that was once viewed as permanent.
—*Curve Magazine*

A heightened awareness of language fuels the series of linked essays as the author looks at social conventions and identity. de Gutes turns to spare, wry, cool, and even-handed prose. Her work is rich and full of heartbreak… through a lighthearted handling of everyday choices from IKEA to clothes to community, de Gutes asks what it means to be human, to be queer, to be straight, to build a life on integrity.
—Monica Drake, *1859: Oregon's Magazine*

D1023921

de Gutes writes about big questions like sexual identity and gender as well as more quotidian problems like the battle against hat head. I particularly appreciated her attention to detail, her wry sense of humor, and her big heart. How could I resist a writer who declares, "I like to believe that I am a lesbian Woody Allen: nervous, neurotic and entirely urban"?

— Geeta Kothari, *Kenyon Review*

Most of the memoirs I love begin with leaving. Leaving usually conjures the sound of tires peeling out on gravel, a fast exit without so much as a glance behind. de Gutes' writing slowly pulls away from the moment of impact, bravely reckoning with the difficult subject of leaving a relationship and her part in what led to its end. She approaches challenging subjects with humor, emotional honesty, and wordplay.

—Kathleen Livingston, *Fourth Genre*

In a word? Bracing. But let me say more: bracing and smart and funny and generous—dangerous, too (just a little, just enough)—and touching, exquisitely so. Full of love and longing and compassion and rue. Kate Carroll de Gutes will have you squirming, snickering (out loud)—savoring her prose (out loud!)—and going back for more. You'll want to get close to this object—this book—again and again.

—Dinah Lenney, author of *The Object Parade*

OBJECTS IN MIRROR ARE CLOSER THAN THEY APPEAR

OBJECTS IN MIRROR ARE CLOSER THAN THEY APPEAR

Kate Carroll de Gutes

Judith Kitchen Select

OVENBIRD

Ovenbird Books, 2015
Port Townsend, WA

This book is published under the Judith Kitchen Select imprint of
Ovenbird Books, a new publishing venture designed to bring literary
nonfiction titles to the attention of the reading public. In the interest
of quality and individuality, Judith Kitchen acts as editor and introduces
each book; the writer has complete autonomy over content and design.

Cover art: Robert Usibelli
Cover design: Geoff Cecil
Author photograph: Jules Hays Norton

Library of Congress Cataloging-in-Publication Data is on file.

ISBN: 1940906121
ISBN-13: 9781940906126
Library of Congress Control Number: 2015904102
Ovenbird Books Port Townsend, WA

For John, Mary, Sue, and Jule,
and the way we always manage
to laugh in the dark.

YOU MAY SEE YOURSELF: AN INTRODUCTION

Objects in Mirror Are Closer Than They Appear is the sixth and last book in Ovenbird's "Judith Kitchen Select" series of innovative literary nonfiction. The Introduction is probably the only thing that Judith left unfinished when she died peacefully after a long illness, on November 6, 2014. She had completed the process of working with Kate while the book was in the final stages of creation. The two carried on an email conversation that was more like a vibrant friendship than an editor-author exchange.

From the time Judith first met Kate at the Rainier Writing Workshop, she was drawn (as was I) to Kate's large personality—witty, inventive, deeply smart, bold, sensitive, always kind—and the way it expresses itself in writing. Smart about gender. Smart about pain. Smart about life. When you have as many sides to your being as this extraordinarily talented and original writer does, this is no mean feat. It requires art. The trick is to draw a line, an arc, to find the living voice in each essay that allows for expansion as well as contraction and control. Proportionality, wildness, revelation, subtlety. And then to find a structure to contain these. This is the sort of challenge Judith thrived on—particularly when the material is so emotionally rich and the writer so capable, brave, and funny. All this the reader is about to discover—if you aren't already a fan of Kate Carroll de Gutes' published, prize-winning essays or have yet to enjoy one of her powerful, entertaining, one-of-a-kind readings.

Judith's words below are from her private correspondence with the author. Let them function in lieu of the Introduction never written. They demonstrate how well the literary partners worked together.

Well, I've read through your order and I think it's working brilliantly. The thrust is backwards, but the tenses keep it fluid and agile—able to take the flashbacks in past tense, the flash forward in future perfect (a brilliant move, and a perfect title), and the several reprises where you either meditate from beyond the actual moment of the piece...(again, that works perfectly). I know I'm familiar with the material, but I see no problems whatsoever with how these pieces go together, building their own kind of momentum.

Also, you need to know that the movement ever backwards is powerful, revealing the sources of tensions that have otherwise simply operated on the previous pieces. You must be so pleased with the way this "works."

I also very much appreciate the shift in person from first to second to third, and the "you" shifts from direct address to a thinly veiled "I" or "one." This, too, adds subtly to the message of identity—just who you are and how comfortable you are in the roles cast upon you. The thing feels virtually seamless…

Honestly, I wouldn't shift a thing…these pieces are really not about your family. They are about you, and your search for sexual identity…

I think you do cover the issues that interest you, and you do give younger women some sense of what it was "like" in an earlier time…I believe the manuscript is working as a book that covers almost everything you've wanted to…It's amazing how we find ways to cover our material even when we're snipping away at it. This is a "statement" without stating it!

The path to self-understanding is always thorny and individual. The shapes behind us that we try to outrun need to be confronted. "Laugh until you cry," the serviceable cliché, is reinvented in Kate's fabulous mirror, as the reader becomes her collaborator. Watch out. You may do both at once. You may see yourself.

—Stan Sanvel Rubin, February 2015

THINGS YOU LEAVE BEHIND

The clay cooker, even though you wish for it multiple times. It seemed ridiculous to store the terracotta dish—wrapped in newsprint in the bottom of a box labeled "Kitchen"—until someday when you again have a kitchen with ample cupboard space.

The electric mixer. It's been so long since you made cookies or a cake yourself that you don't even think about this until the day you are trying to bake Christmas cookies and must use your immersion blender to try to cream the butter and sugar together.

The toaster, the blender, and the electric rice cooker. You thought you'd be coming back and then finally when you weren't you'd already purchased two out of the three.

The crock pot, the coffee maker, and the Cuisinart. You really only miss the last, but you don't have the space to store an appliance that you use six times a year.

The couch, the Morris chair, the buffet, the beds, and the desk your father bought you. You do take your grandmother's dresser and the hutch, though.

The TV, the stereo, and the hot tub (because they all seem impractical for a third-floor walkup).

Your history. Although this isn't strictly true. You carry that with you, the good, the bad, the quotidian. You have within you that late summer night in 2006 when you lit a fire in the clay chiminea on the patio and the two of you sat drinking gin and tonics, eating Caprese salad, and talking about not much, glad simply to rest in each other's company and the waning fingernail of a moon. And you carry that solstice: all the candles burning with their yellow light, nestled against fir boughs that you and the dog had gathered up on your morning walks; you went to bed after a meal flooded with wine and woke the next morning moments before the candle flames would have touched their fiery tongues to the evergreen needles. You hold the death of grandparents and the arrhythmias, heart attacks, and heart block of parents. You did not leave the memory of putting down your first black-and-white cat. Or the second. Or the tiny grey one you used to carry around the neighborhood in your Carhartt jacket because he was too weak to walk. You take with you the walks through Pike Place, the men shouting and throwing fish, the two of you with your heads thrown back in laughter. You keep that vacation on Ross Lake with the Adirondack chairs and the moon on the Canadian boundary waters; you were both very tranquil on that trip and you can still call up that quiet sometimes.

You chose not to take the material objects, but they were just artifacts of your marriage anyway. The real things you could never leave behind.

LIFE RAFT WITH RANDOM SPOONS

I don't think about it much. I try not to remember the time she forgot why she was driving west on US 101 towards Port Angeles, Washington, on her way to pick up my sister at the small regional airport which only opened for the two flights a day arriving from Seattle. When my mom tells me she doesn't own an answering machine and has never used her Roku box before, I calmly explain that she does and she has. And when she tells me that driving wouldn't be a problem, I ask her to show me her cellphone and how to turn it on.

"I have a cellphone? Where?"

This conversation occurs at least three times a week.

But I cannot ignore the paperwork on my desk: Durable Powers of Attorney. The right hand corner of each of the nine pages is initialed MCD in blue pen. Midway down the first page is Article 3: "At such time as necessary, I designate Kathleen Carroll de Gutes as my attorney-in-fact." Next to this is a letter from the neurologist declaring my mother incapable of handling legal and financial affairs. May you never have to ask a doctor for a letter like this or hear the diagnosis, "Dementia with no behavioral disturbances."

⇌ ⇌

After the seventh call, I stop tallying. It's always the same. "Are you sure I can't take my bookcase with me?"

We are moving my mother from a remote 2,200 square foot house outside the Olympic National Forest in Sequim, Washington, to a 500 square foot, one bedroom apartment in an assisted living facility in Portland, Oregon. My mother already decreed that every piece of framed art will come. She is moving two 3'x2' green velvet matted paintings of Greek temples—or are they Roman?, six paintings of Cothele "house"—our forebears' English castle—43 framed family photos plus one oil painting of my great-great grandmother, my great-great grandfather's pocket watches mounted on black velvet, my great grandmother's lace fan shadowboxed in a gold gilt frame, a spoon display case with sterling spoons—never silver plate—collected by

my grandmother—Or, maybe these are random spoons?—
The sterling silver baby spoons of my mother and her brother, and my grandmother and her sisters. I'm not sure.

The truth is, I stopped listening to the story of these
objects a long time ago. I don't know who gave my parents
the sterling silver Revere bowl (nor why it's called that),
only that it was the first wedding present they received.
I've forgotten if the green and white plates are Spode or
Copeland, only that we use them for Christmas dinner
and that they were possibly bequeathed by my great-grandmother Carroll to my grandmother. I am sure, however,
that my grandmother had so much china that these plates
were reserved solely for Chinese takeout dinners. If I ask
my mother about this or any other item—from the Stiffel
lamp given to her by her mother-in-law ("I always thought
it was something cheap," she said when I was rewiring it.
"Are you sure it says 'Stiffel'? If so, that was your grandfather's doing. He knew quality."), to the cast iron Cossack
brought back by her father from World War I's Eastern
Front, to the rusted aluminum vegetable peeler she got at
a bridal shower hosted by her mother's bridge club—she
can tell me the provenance of any one of these things. I've
heard the stories so many times and there are so many
items that I can no longer catalog them all, if I ever could.
But what my mother cannot tell me is her address, where
she lived last, or the day, month, and year.

I take the quarter-sawn oak table and chairs, and the buffet. Sue gets the cherry wood dressing table. Jule collects the artichoke plates, glass salad plates, and Spode dessert plates. I also amass 14 additional place settings of Wedgwood to "fill out the rest of my hutch," while Sue takes the rest of the Lennox. We leave the gold-rimmed Limoges bowls specified only for creamed onions and only at Thanksgiving and Christmas.

To my mother's chagrin, we leave the 9'x8' bookcase, the Baldwin spinet, one Lennox lamp, and a clock that was carried from Bowdoin, Maine, to New Richmond, Wisconsin in 1867. This ornate, gothic-looking parlor clock has been in a closet for the past 32 years, ever since my grandmother died. About a month after my mother settled in Portland, she called me, crying, asking if I'd sold the clock. I tell her it's in a box in my garage.

"Well I want it. Bring it over."

It was a calculated lie on my part and I can only hope my mother won't remember asking for it.

My mother is not holding onto these items and their stories—mentally, I mean—because they reside in the last bulwark before total mental oblivion. She itemizes them and recites their stories as she always has done, as if beautiful objects can make a beautiful life. As if the Carroll silver service with Gorham hallmarks and the avant-garde C engraved on the coffeepot, creamer, and sugar dish will mitigate the effects of an alcoholic husband; as if remembering who sent the silver compote as a wedding present could help call up the breathless belief of beginning a new life with her beloved; as if past and provenance attenuate present pity.

—◄— —►—

She cannot remember helping us sort through and pack up her house. In fact, during the entire process, she sat on the dove grey leather couch in the great room, sleeping through hours of daytime television while my sisters and I boxed up everything we thought she'd need in assisted living. By need, I mean everything she frantically wanted to hold on to. I imagine her bobbing in a sea of the flotsam and jetsam that makes up a life, arms wrapped around the pigeon-hole desk she found in my great-great grandfather's attic, or the spool bed that my great-grandfather was born and died in, or the wing-back chair she took from my grandmother's basement and re-upholstered. She knows these items, she knows their stories, and she knows her own story with them: where she first encountered the cane chair that goes with the desk, how old her kids were when she first recovered the chair, where she found the store that specially made the mattress for the spool bed. As my mother increasingly forgets that she lives in Portland or that she just ate a meal—"I'm so hungry, when are we having dinner?"—these objects do become a life raft, something to grasp onto in the face of terrible storms.

I wish I'd understood this more completely when we were preparing my mother for her move. The least object—a broken spoon rest, the kitchen soap dispenser, swapping out Handiwipes for an Ocello sponge—makes a difference in her orientation. I wish I had driven the eight-hour round trip one last time and loaded the second end table and the other Lennox lamp. Yet, here is the curio cabinet with 113 ornamental elephants in brass, ivory, glass, and stone. There is the washstand with the hand-painted porcelain picture of my great-grandmother. Across the room is a window seat transformed into a shelf full of rustic art—pre-Columbian "dolls" from Mexico, a pot from Peru, polished ammonite fossils, and a rock that opens to reveal a fossilized trilobite. Above the kitchen sink hangs a red-matted picture of a farm, the bucolic scene in a frame of reclaimed barn wood.

"Why did you bring that?" my mother interrogates. "I don't care about that!"

"Because, Mother," the words fall out breathy and tired. "You told me you couldn't have a kitchen without this picture."

"I told you that?" A hazy sort of look passes over her eyes, clouding them over.

"Mom, you know you helped us pack, right?"

Tears are streaming down her face. She shakes her head.

"Where do you think you were when we packed you up?"

"Warehoused somewhere so it was easier."

⚊⧾ ⧾⚊

These objects, and the stories that keep them alive, are permanent in a life where nothing else is or was. My mother's father may have died when she was only 6 years old, but here in a dresser drawer are Raggedy Ann and Raggedy Andy, their cloth skin darkened with age to the color of weak tea. Andy's shirt is missing its buttons, Ann's hair matted and fading from red to rose.

"Mom, what about these?"

The tears come as fast as the words. "Oh, no, no, no, please. That's the last thing my father bought for me."

Later, she tells me that her father had to borrow money in order to buy my grandmother a ticket to visit him in Illinois where he was working for the war effort. If she makes the connection that the dolls were probably purchased with borrowed funds, she doesn't say so. Over 72 years, the dolls move from one dresser to another, and then from one house to another, then finally to the assisted living facility.

Five months post-move, my mom asks about her Marghab linen. Most of the linen was her mother's, brought back from pre-World War II Portugal.

"I suppose you sold all that." It's a declaration.

"Well, except for the hand towels you brought here."

My mother looks angry, then sad. "All that linen."

"Mom, what would we have done with it? It made you money."

"I suppose. You put them out as hand towels and then somebody actually uses them and you're mad and never invite them over again."

For this reason, my mother's and grandmother's Marghab remained in thin, flat boxes, wrapped carefully in archival tissue paper that kept the linen from yellowing. It was there in those boxes, proof of a trip to Portugal, proof of a genteel lifestyle. Why wouldn't we want to keep these boxes in our own dressers and inherited buffets until it is time for our caregivers—all three daughters are childless—to sell in our own estate sales the linen saved for three generations? I can't explain to my mother in a way that makes sense to her, why we wouldn't want that. Instead, I go home and take another load of my own unused items to Goodwill.

WEDDING RING

I have a black-and-white photograph of us in the green leather Morris chair that we bought because I was in love with all things Mission style. The picture was taken in the mid-90s back before either of us was very grey. You are sitting on my lap, your long, skinny legs draped across the arm of the chair. My head is resting back against the leather and I have a contented, sly smile on my face and my eyes are sparkling. You are nuzzling my neck and smiling a big smile, all your teeth showing. This picture—matted and framed—used to hang on our bedroom wall. After you took it down, you gave it to me and said, "I thought we would always be this way."

I am alone, now, in this chair, in this house that used to be mine, and I am sitting across from your new husband.

Last week, the two of you got married in Mexico, but no one knows that except for me. And I am not supposed to know. But you have told me I can drop by to pick up some mail because Eric is at the house. Sitting on the couch, in fact, and wearing a big gold band on his left ring finger.

After a minute of talking, he realizes that he is wearing the ring. I'm not sure if he knows I've seen it. He laces his hands behind his head, not an incongruous pose for a good ol' boy from Payette, Idaho who collects guns, drives a big Dodge Ram, and voted for George W. Bush (twice). I stay talking to him a while longer—mostly just to see what he'll do. Will he hold this pose for more than five minutes? He doesn't move. His legs are resting on the coffee table and a laptop sits on his thighs between his beer belly and his knees.

Finally, I go into the kitchen, the one we remodeled together in 1997, and pick up my mail. When I stick my head back into the living room to say goodbye, his hands are tucked under his laptop. I wish I had said, "Gee, you're supposed to place your hands *on* the keys, not *under* them." But the thing is, I like this guy, and I knew this day was coming. I told everyone I thought you two were going to get engaged in Mexico. You just went a step further. I say nothing to you. You are not my wife any longer.

When you finally announce the news on New Year's Eve, letting me know, as well, I tell you this story. You say, "I know, he kept forgetting to take it off. Silly boy."

THINGS YOU SAVE

T in foil pressed as smooth as possible.
  Rubber bands bound into a bigger and bigger ball.

The card your mother wrote you on your 21st birthday, her handwriting illegible but not shaky and spidery like it is in the card she writes 21 years later for your 42nd birthday, three days before her third thoracic surgery.

Poems you wrote to your wife in college. You'll sift through them later like an archeologist looking for clues about a devastated civilization.

Cards you gave to and then saved for your wife, figuring someday she'd want them. You placed them carefully under her summer shirts, third drawer down. She finds them, along with the last birthday card her grandmother sent (you saved that for her, too), the summer before you leave. She runs her finger along the top card before returning them to the bottom of the drawer, hidden again until some spring day after you've gone.

Receipts from six weeks of hotel rooms and meals during your mother's first hospitalization, along with boarding passes from Southwest Airlines and Amtrak, and $275 of gas receipts, all stuffed into a manila envelope labeled "mother."

Your mother's life. This makes you believe you can save anything, which turns out not to be true.

SEISMOLOGY

I like to believe that I am a lesbian Woody Allen: nervous, neurotic, and entirely urban. That if I get too far away from an espresso machine or a WiFi signal for my smartphone, I will die. Or, if not die, suffer severe cramping. I do not want to have to kill a cockroach (beseeching me with its freakishly large, Precious Moments-like eyes), or use a Katadyne filter to purify water gathered from some desert cenote, or carry super glue and adhesive tape for both mechanical and human breakdowns. I want to sleep in my Sleep Number bed (65 at night when I'm lying on my side, 35 in the morning when I'm on my back) behind my double-locked apartment doors on the third floor of a secure building. In the morning, I want to walk to the coffee shop on the corner, drink some fresh-squeezed orange juice and a double-tall, half-caff, non-fat latte, and read the *New York Times*. Later, if it's not too much, I might catch a bus downtown to see my Jungian therapist, or the streetcar into Northwest to see my hypnotherapist.

Instead, I am driving on Mexico Highway 1. At night. In a tiny, butt-dragger of a car, the Nissan Tsuru. Oh, and I'm not wearing my glasses. They're back at the condo where my new girlfriend and I are staying for the next two weeks.

"Um, why aren't these people moving over for us," I say at the exact moment that both Katrina and I realize what is actually going on. "I'm pulling over," I say calmly, as I drive the Tsuru over a curb and into what we now realize is the median. "Jesus Christ! We were going the wrong way on the most dangerous highway in Mexico!" Now that the car is stopped, neuroses kick in.

We collect ourselves and then must drive nine more kilometers down the correct lane of Highway 1 to the road that leads to our condo. The road is unmarked, a left turn across traffic, at night. This particular stretch of highway is full of semis making trips from Loreto to La Paz and back again. There are signs posted every half kilometer or so that say, *No rebase con raya continua.* Do not pass when there is a solid line. And so the semis bear down on our little Nissan Tsuru. We are driving slowly, looking for the unmarked, unlit road that leads to our condo and we have on our left turn signal. As we later learn, this is a sign to the vehicle behind that it is okay to pass even though the *raya* is *continua*.

When we finally turn left, an air horn echoes as the truck behind us screeches past. We fishtail into the dirt at the side of our unmarked road. Katrina has been holding a dozen eggs on a flat that we picked up at Loreto's only *supermercado* and, as we skid off the road for a second time—death no less imminent than when we were travelling the wrong way—an egg flies from the flat on her lap and breaks on the floor of the car and oozes over her flip flops and feet.

We have been in the Baja for three hours.

⇥⇤

During the two weeks we stay in Loreto, we are only caught driving after sundown one other time. Of course, it is the time we have travelled 28 kilometers over an unmarked dirt road that wends its way through the Sierra de Gigante mountains outside Loreto. A road full of blind curves and hairpin turns; a dirt road with no guard rail and a shoulder crumbling thousands of feet (okay, *several* hundred feet) to the arroyo below where there is no clearing for a life flight helicopter. We'd been trying to reach the mission at San Javier. The Spanish built this mission between the Pacific and the Gulf in 1699, but later abandoned it because the Indians, who were getting along just fine without the Holy Trinity, kept killing the Jesuits. Built from stone quarried from the bed of the Santo Domingo brook 20 km south-east of San Javier, the mission is a well-preserved example of Spanish baroque architecture and is situated in a lush oasis of coconut and date palms and orange trees. At least, that is what the Internet says.

Because we will be visiting a church, my inamorata has showered, shaved her legs, and put on a sleeveless shirt and a printed skirt. On her feet are blue flip flops embroidered with shells and daisies. The white and coral accents of the flip flops nicely complement her lime green pedicure. I should also mention that she has artfully draped a pashmina over her shoulders for warmth. Because we are climbing to 3600 feet in mountains called the Sierras.

I am wearing shorts—blue and purple plaid—a clean blue t-shirt, and purple Teva sandals. Never let it be said that lesbians don't coordinate their outfits or favor only Birkenstocks. Of course, Katrina will also roll her eyes in exasperation if I don't tell you that I do NOT have a pashmina. Or a polar fleece. In fact, as we continue to climb through cooling air, I am forced to wear one of her black cardigans that we happen to have in the car. It is two sizes too small and has ruined my retro-Midwest look.

We've made two big errors on this drive. First, we started out for San Javier at 3:45 p.m. and, in December, in the Baja, it is fully dark by 5:45 p.m. We could have easily driven the 24 km out and back in this time except, as a sign warned us multiple times before the pavement ended and the gravel begins, *Este camino no es alta velocidad.* Well, no kidding. We're averaging about 12 km per hour on the *camino del muerto* and that's probably faster than we should be driving. The second mistake we've made is that we did not set our odometer the minute we turned onto the road of death so we have no idea how far we've travelled. We could be only 5 km from the mission, but it might as well be 50 because it is 5:10 and total darkness descends in 35 minutes.

I should mention that I wanted to turn around the minute the pavement ended, a scant 20 minutes from our condo. At that point, it was 4:05, but Katrina—deftly maneuvering the Tsuru around oil-pan-ripping boulders, high-centering ruts, and lug-nut-loosening washboard—laughed at me. "Baby, we're fine," she said and patted my leg. "This is a good road. Don't you think this is a good road? It's wide, it's well marked. It's a good road."

Yes, I thought, compared to Panama or the jungles of Colombia, this is a good road. "But you're in a skirt and flip flops," I said.

She smiled at me and that's when I noticed she'd also put on lipstick. "Honey, nothing's going to happen."

Right on cue, a rock hit the undercarriage of the car and I started expounding on the dangers of ripping out our oil pan or puncturing a cooling line or blowing out a tire. Then I said again, trying to appeal to the part of her that likes to dress up and be pretty, "You're in a skirt and flip flops."

This was, I believe, what both of my very urban therapists would call a "learning moment." Had I been with my ex-wife of 20-plus years, no moment would have been necessary. I'd have been driving and would have simply turned the car around. And given her fear of heights, she'd have taken one look at the crumbling road edge and agreed. But Katrina has much less fear than the average woman—or man—and, as I was "learning," saw nothing wrong with changing a flat on an unpaved mountain road while wearing a skirt and flip flops.

"We don't have a flashlight. We don't even know if the car has a spare. And if we rip out the oil pan, we'll have to walk back in the dark."

Ultimately, we agreed to drive until 5:10 p.m. and if we didn't reach the mission, turn around. It seemed an excellent compromise between a woman who ran a raft down the Colorado on a whim and a woman who would run, if forced, to catch a bus or streetcar (*if* it was raining and *if* no coffee shops were nearby where one could wait for a taxi).

⇥ ⇤

At 5:10, we pulled over next to a beautiful pond that reflected the mountains in the waning light. It looked like an oasis on a Hollywood set, water lapping against a red rocky outcropping that dripped with green plants. Further back, away from the water, saguaro cacti stood with their arms in the air, cheering our decision to turn around.

"I feel like the mission is really close. Can we just go up to that next bend in the road?" Katrina smiled at me and I thought about how nice her quince colored lips looked against her white teeth.

Like an idiot, I agreed. "But we are absolutely, positively turning around at 5:15, Katrina."

"Yes. We're turning around at 5:15, Baby."

"I'm serious."

"I see that," she said, and patted my leg again.

By 5:15, we rounded two more curves, but still did not see the mission. Katrina stopped the car and looked straight ahead, her hands on the steering wheel at 10 and 2.

"It goes against my spirit of adventure to turn around," she said.

I didn't mention banditos, or that we only had about 200 pesos in bribe money, or that I was not carrying a passport.

"But you're right. It makes sense to turn around." She sighed and turned the car east, back towards the Gulf of Mexico and the city of Loreto.

Now I could finally relax and enjoy the amazing scenery. Every place there was no ground water, agave, Joshua tree, piñon pine, and cacti grew. But along the river bottom, there were date palms, coconut palms, citrus trees, and oleander in bloom. The Sierra de Gigante looked impossibly angular and the fading light changed the mountains' color from red to brown to black. I was enjoying myself so much, I didn't even gloat when we had to swerve around a muffler lying in the middle of road which had not been there on our drive in.

⤜⟦ ⟧⤛

Three months later, I am back in Mexico, driving alone on Highway 1 from Cabo San Lucas to Todos Santos, ninety minutes north along the Pacific Coast. The sere landscape feels familiar to me and I am relaxed behind the wheel. Still, there are moments when I think I should be worried, or at least less nonchalant, acting like I am not some old hand at Mexican highways. Maybe I am a *little* nervous, but I'm also feeling a bit full of myself after negotiating customs, renting a car, and not having an accident when I saw the Applebee's, McDonald's, Home Depot, and Costco on the outskirts of Cabo. To keep my focus, I chant the road signs as I pass them: *Por seguridad todos, dismaynua su velocidad; Si toma no maneje; Obedezca los señales.* For everyone's safety, slow down; Don't drink and drive; Obey the signs.

It seems tourists are the only people who actually obey *los señales.* Still, I arrive in Todos Santos without an accident or even a near miss and park the car for 3 days, steeling myself for the drive into Playa Las Palmas—a pristine, empty beach accessible only by a drive across desert sands and then a hike through a palm grove so lush and giant it reminds me of *Land of the Lost.*

Bob, my host in Todos Santos, gives me directions to the beach that are a bit sketchy and rambling, as are most

27

things outside Cabo, Baja's official tourist zone. "First, travel south to kilometer marker 59, turn off the highway onto the road shoulder, and drive back along the side of the road toward traffic. Then take the first left that appears to head into the desert. The sign above the road says, *road closed*, but just ignore it. That sign's been there since the 70s. Make sure when you turn off the road you turn right. Don't turn left towards the house with the *Pescado Muerto* sign."

"But I thought you said to turn left?"

"Into the desert, yes. Not off the highway, though. Anyways, you'll be okay. Just keep driving sort of fast because your car can get stuck in soft sand if you're moving too slowly. It's a dirt road, but it's a good road. So, keep driving until you can't go any farther. Then get out and walk until you hit the beach."

I was supposed to take this trip with my ex-wife. It was going to be our way of reconnecting after a terrible year of financial devastation and caretaking for my catastrophically ill mother. Instead, we separated and postponed the trip, thinking we'd work things out and take it at a later date. Now, 18 months later, I am here alone. I'm not unhappy about it, the being alone in Mexico, but I am pounded by grief over the end of the relationship. I cannot excuse myself for leaving her like a discarded muffler by the side of our road, and I hope being in this place where the desert meets the sea will help me find some sort of forgiveness in myself, for myself.

I walk around unable to believe I am here. Ten years earlier, 5 years earlier, I don't think I could have done this. I kept saying I wanted to travel alone, but the reality was: I was too afraid to go. My fears were myriad—from what if I have an asthma attack in a foreign country (read: and die alone) to what if I break some law and am arrested, beaten up, and thrown in jail (and die alone in a dark prison cell)? What if I get bad food poisoning and need a doctor (and the doctor doesn't speak English and I really have eColi 0157:H7 and my kidneys shut down and I die alone on a gurney in a foreign hospital)? What if I get caught in a rip tide and pulled out to sea (and don't drown immediately, but rather bob around for a few days—dehydrated and delirious— until I am finally ripped apart by sharks and die alone)?

I used to think these fears were the byproduct of too much television, but I quit TV and the fears persisted. So I decided it was because I knew what I had accomplished was all smoke and mirrors. Maybe we all think that about ourselves at some level—that it's just a lucky break that gets us the affordable Edwardian in the gentrified neighborhood, or a chance roll of the dice that we don't have inoperable melanoma. At some level, maybe we are all really waiting for the mortgage default notice, the call back for a second mammogram, the pink slip, the overdraft notice. But in my case, fear kept me paralyzed.

⋗⋘ ⋙⋖

The drive across the desert to the beach surprises me because I haven't really planned it, worried about it, or figured out contingencies for scenarios A, B, and F. Instead, I get in my Chevy Aveo rental car without much of a thought for what could go wrong, and begin driving over the shifting sands in a 2-wheel drive sedan.

I am doing this and I am not worrying about sudden cardiac arrest or an asthma attack. I am not worrying about getting the rental car caught on soft sand—well, I'm not worrying *very much* about this. I tell myself that I'm fine. I actually say out loud, "This is a good road." I say that I am on an adventure, that the worst that can happen is that I'll have to hike to the highway for help or to town, which is only 8 km away. Then I remind myself that I am carrying a liter of water, two meals, and a long-sleeved shirt.

But mostly, I am not thinking at all. I am simply driving past mesquite and saguaro towards an oasis rich with coco and date palms, taking in the scenery. It is the only thing I can do. I don't have any distractions—television or movies or the Internet (well, no more than once a day at the Internet café). I don't have a reliable cell connection. All I have is a rental car, a journal, and the books I've brought with me—*Anna Karenina* with its story of failing marriages and a book about projection by a Jungian psychologist. I hope these books are exactly what I need to understand that things can go wrong in the best of circumstances.

Without anything to really distract me, there is nothing to do except feel my uncomfortable and neurotic thoughts and recognize them for what they are. Of course I *could* be attacked by marauding Mexicans who drop on zip lines from the palm trees, steal my car, and leave me in the desert tied to a cactus like the old man in that episode of *Kung Fu*, but the likelihood of that is *really quite slim*.

Still, this is somewhat of a revelation for me.

On that trip to Loreto, I learned that if I was physically active—paddling a kayak in moderate surf, say—that my brain could only focus on that one thing. Navigating around a point without crashing into the rocky cliffs took my full attention, and for 7 or 10 minutes—however long it took—I was blessedly free of fear and worry and guilt, the three emotions that travel with me like unwelcome siblings. Here in Todos Santos I cannot kayak because the surf is too rough. But I can drive to the beach and hike and sit on the shore as waves 8, 10, and 12 feet tall crash down, the drama of nature drowning out the drama of me. I'm a little surprised that all it takes is some white noise to quiet my head. I hope that I am not becoming one of those people you see walking through the city wearing Bose Noise Cancelling Headphones. But even this I would do in order to keep this feeling, because for the first time in my life, who—and what—I am seems possible.

DON WE NOW OUR GAY APPAREL

Through the years I will own a heather-blue, wool ski cap that itches my head and causes my forehead to welt; a black polar fleece fez which will sit high on my head but leave my ears cold and exposed, and me looking like some Ukrainian refugee. The fez will have flaps which come down and cover the back of my neck and ears, but then I will look like an Appalachian refugee—and a cold Ukrainian trumps a warm, back-holler hillbilly any day. I also will have a brown knit skull cap that my wife will make for me one winter when we will be trapped inside by an ice storm and there isn't anything else to do and besides, I will need a cap when we can go back outside again. Finally, in the center console of the second truck I will own will be a blue, polar fleece ski cap that I buy at Old Navy because it is only $5 and I will figure if I am ever stranded, I can wear it while I wait for rescue.

Mostly, I will never wear these hats. They will sit in a dresser in the basement ready for the inevitable day of really cold weather—which in Portland, Oregon comes once a year, in December or February, when the city gets a requisite day of snow. But here is what I will learn after I get divorced: that if I wear a hat and gloves when it is even slightly cold or raining outside, I won't mind being out so much, and I might even enjoy it. This might seem like common sense to you and something I should not have to wait 44 years to figure out. Maybe you are an adult on the East coast who has been wearing a hat all your life. Or maybe you live in Denver or Jackson or Bend and know that 60% of a body's heat loss is through the head. I probably learned this, too, but I am also told that I don't look good in hats—particularly ski caps (will they even be called this in 2009?). My mother tells me only boys wear these types of hats. I don't know what she says girls wear, but I'm sure she thinks it should be something stylish and jaunty, worn high on the brow (not pulled down low like a Neanderthal or a serial killer), a hat that just grazes the tops of the ears. The problem with a hat like this is that they stopped making them in 1958—well, except for berets, but I am told I

don't look good in these, either. And besides, only preten-
tious writers wear berets.

But, in 2008, I will get divorced and truly embrace my
sexuality, and then I will realize that the reason I never
wore a hat was because I thought they made me look
butch. Which I was, am, will always be. But it will take a
girl embracing this in me to make me understand that not
only is it okay to look like a big old lesbian in a Carhartt
jacket and a polar fleece hat, it is preferable to looking like
a cold and miserable lesbian who scowls and complains
whenever she has to go outside in the winter.

It also will take 21st century hair products for me to embrace hats. Before, when severely inclement weather forced
me to wear a hat in order to avoid contracting pneumonia,
my head would heat up and my fine, thin hair would lose
what little body my gel or hairspray imparted, and stick
flat against my head, making me look like a 12-year-old
boy. But with 21st century hair powders and glues and poly-
mer gels, I will be able to take a hat off, palm the top of my
head, and reconstitute my hair.

One winter after my divorce I will be in Central Washington,
hiking over the frozen Columbia plateau. It will be so cold
I will think, *I'll just grab that blue cap out of the truck and slide
it over my noggin. I'm out here alone tromping over buff-colored
grass that's so frozen it's not even cracking under foot, and it*

seems ridiculous not to wear a hat. So even though the navy blue will not be the exact right blue to complement my black Carhartt gasoline jacket (with quilted arms and a blanket lining), I will snatch the hat and pull it on. It will cover my ears and sit so low on my forehead that it will almost touch the outer edges of my eyebrows. But it will do the trick. I will start to warm up.

Then I will do something surprising—take a picture of myself. I will feel warm and happy—a rare day free of the millstone of "should" that hangs around my neck. The landscape in its sparseness will fill me with quiet. Freezing fog will have covered the bare branches of the Garry oak trees, turning them into land-based coral, and the Ponderosa pines will look like flocked Christmas trees. Between the white ice, grey fog, and the dark of the trunks, branches, and my Carhartt coat, the world will look like a black-and-white photo. My red Irish cheeks and my blue cap will be the only spots of color in the picture, and I actually will like the way they stand out in the photo. Like it so much that I will do another surprising thing: I will upload the picture to my Facebook page. It will not occur to me that my friends might comment on the picture, but they do. No one will say I look like a Neanderthal, a serial killer, or a ball-buster. No one will say, "Where did you get that ugly hat?"

INDIAN SUMMER

I t is a beautiful November day, the sky blue with pale yellow light, warm enough that my father and I are not wearing coats as we walk down the gangplank to the USS Blueback, a decommissioned diesel submarine that is anchored on the east shore of the Willamette River across from downtown Portland. Less than a week from now he will be diagnosed with Stage IVb metastatic esophageal cancer, but today all we know is that he has a tumor in his throat and that it's cancerous but not too big. Still, my dad believes it is a "death sentence." Then again, with every ache and pain that's ever lasted for more than an hour he's said, "I hope it's not the Big C, Kaydoos." It's hard to feel compassionate. I mean, he's been waiting for this moment since I was 10 years old, and he was younger than I am now.

My father has wanted to tour this submarine ever since he spotted it four years ago. Every time he has come to visit he asks if this is the time we can go see it, please, it would really make him happy, please can we tour that submarine, Kaydoos. Every time I say, "Not this time, Dad." I say no for a variety of reasons: because I will have to take time off work; because I already have taken months off work to care for my mother because he wouldn't or couldn't or both; because, quite honestly, I am perpetually angry at him and I don't really want to do anything that feels as if it is above and beyond normal filial duties.

But here we are.

He called me up before he left home and said, "Listen, Kaydoos, do you think we could visit that submarine when I come down, you know, given my condition?"

I thought, *he is using his cancer to manipulate me,* and then I still fell for it. How could I not? Who wants to refuse a request from a 72-year-old man with cancer? I am his own personal Make-A-Wish Foundation.

When he joined the Navy, it was because he wanted to be a submariner, but the brass had different plans and told him he didn't qualify. I don't know why he wanted to serve on a windowless metal tube under the water and I don't know if he's ever even seen the inside of one. There are a lot of questions that I have never asked.

We board the vessel, descending a flight of narrow metal stairs, and I notice how lumbering and careful he is at the same time. My father is—well, not tiny—but I think the cancer must have been eating at him for a while because he seems weak even though it must take a lot of muscle to haul around all that weight. Coming down the gangplank, he said his legs felt like rubber and we stopped twice so he could rest. If he falls in this submarine, in one of these narrow passages, I don't know how we'll get him out. But once below deck, he's like an excited boy. He fires off a list of questions: Is this a skipjack hull? Single or double hull? Are the engines made by Norton Grumman? What's the test depth? Did our guide know that the Russian Typhoon class submarine can stay submerged for six months at a time? Are the torpedoes wire-guided?

He points out to me the sonar room and the Christmas tree—the green and red lit panel that controls the ballast. We peer through the periscope and see traffic racing by on the freeway four stories above. We look at the mess hall and a Thanksgiving menu from 1969 that includes cigarettes for dessert. He tries to get me to lie down on a coffin-like bunk that is only 20 inches wide and 18 inches below the next bunk and laughs when I refuse and gasp for breath just at the thought of the tight space.

As we climb the stairs again to exit, I bring up the rear, hoping that if he falters, I will be able to break his fall. We both notice a blue line painted across one riser and, below it, the words: "Water Line." He reaches down and scoops his wrist towards the stair, his big index finger pointing at the words."You see that, Kaydoos? Can you believe how far underwater we've been?"

THE NEW NORMAL

In the window of a corner room, on the third floor of the Heathman Hotel, my father sits alone in an overstuffed chair. He's here in this expensive, luxury hotel because my therapist has forbidden him from staying with my wife and me in our Edwardian home just across the river.

This therapist said to me, "If you won't tell him, Kate, I will."

It's the first time she has ever delivered an iron-clad edict. Normally, I go see the Jungian and wander around the ephemeral, amorphous world of my dreams, trying to tie the chainsaws skittering across the floor of a dream cabin to my waking life. It's perfect for the writer in me—and for sidling up to issues on the oblique. The result is—or rather has been—an easy-going therapist who encourages art and massage, and not hard phone calls in which I tell my father I've booked and paid for four nights at the Heathman. That he'll retire there each evening after visiting his wife in the nursing home 1.25 miles from my house.

"It's not very normal to put your dad in a hotel for the holidays," he said.

"Yeah," I snap back in a moment of uncharacteristic toughness, "well get used to it. Because this is the new normal."

So there he is. In the floral chair, a single cup French press atop the round, Queen Anne side table. Magically, because this is Portland, Oregon and not Portland, Maine, flurries of snow fall and whirl around, caught between the updraft created by the Heathman and John Helmer Haberdasher located just across Salmon Street. My dad can look down into the store's window and see Irish wool caps, fedoras, a stack of Pendleton shirts, the merest glimpse of a rainbow fan of silk ties. And on the street below, the Meier and Frank Christmas parade complete with Santa in his sleigh. I have no doubt that this is the life my father imagined for himself. The life he did, in fact, lead for a few years—staying at The Dukes in London, buying suits tailor-made for him on Saville Row. So, to be in a position such as this at the end of his life is a grace.

He walks over to Helmer's, intending to get an Irish walking cap. Does he remember the one I returned with from Donegal, Ireland? But Helmer's cap is $135 and that's too much for an elderly pensioner with a wife in a nursing home, an elderly pensioner trying to recover from his lack of financial sense. Years earlier, when money had not seemed finite or worrisome, my father appeared not to think twice about the handmade shirts with mono-grammed cuffs or the silk ties cut the correct length for his prodigious gut. Tobias Tailors, established in 1889 at 32 Saville Row, London, made his three-piece blue pin-stripe suit, a dove grey one, and two tuxedos: one black, the other white. I'm sure there were more, but these suits, all size 50 regular, were the ones my father kept and were the ones I took for myself when I cleaned out their house after he died.

When I was younger, my father's Royall Bay Rhum and Royall Bay Lyme aftershave bottles captivated me. Their tiny pewter caps fashioned to look like a crown; the brown bottles with the fragrance name in raised letters on the glass called to mind a dandy mixing up his own scent in whatever bottle he found handy in his new Bahamian fron-tier, a way to maintain civility even as he colonized and sub-dued a new set of natives; the packaging connoted kitchen chemistry and a make-do ethic, years before reduce, re-cycle, reuse became an ethos for the DIY crowd; and the brand story on the parchment-colored label appealed to a young butch not yet jaded by the marketing of J. Peterman or Restoration Hardware. Taken as a whole, the aftershave seemed to hold some secret. To what, I wasn't sure. I'm still not sure. I only know I loved the scent and the packaging, and I waited impatiently for my father to finish a bottle so I could then have it for myself.

Maybe he felt the same way. I don't know why he loved those two scents, so different from each other. One fresh, bright, and citrusy, the other pungent and oily, smelling of bay leaves and menthol. My mother loved the way he smelled in them, is that why he liked them? Or did he like them because they were initially sold only by Brooks Brothers and the very act of purchasing them made him feel distinguished? Did he get his first bottle there? Or when he and my mother went to Caneel Bay?

At $65, a bottle of Royall Bay Rhum or Royall Bay Lyme cost less than half of the Irish walking cap. I wonder how my dad felt running his fingers over the rough tweed of the cap—wanting so much to be able to buy the items that to him signified success. I have no doubt he looked at the price of the hat first—he always did. I can imagine him tossing the hat back down, not even trying it on his grey, thinning pate. But this can't be true because I remember him telling me that one of the things he loved about John Helmer's was that they stocked hats that fit him. I don't know what size he wore—I think a 7 5/8. I do know he returned from the shop angry because of the prices. Underneath the anger, I suppose, was disappointment and shame that he could no longer peel off a hundred from his wallet and outfit himself like a proper gentleman.

The next day, he returned to the haberdasher and purchased a bottle of Royall Bay Lyme. I can see him going back to his corner room on the third floor of the Heathman, sitting in the chair, and waiting for the electric kettle to boil water for his afternoon coffee. In my vision, it is still snowing outside and he sits watching the dry powder accumulate on the sidewalk, and listening as the water starts to boil.

The last time my father stayed at the Heathman, he knew it was the last time. He had cancer that would kill him in less than six months, just like John Helmer, Jr. who would die of a cancer recurrence a year after my father. Both men had prostate cancer, although it was Stage IVb esophageal cancer with metastases that killed my dad. But my parents still made the trip to Portland to spend Thanksgiving with me.

I wish I could say I was compassionate during that last visit. But the truth is, my father had been waiting for cancer his whole life. "Oh, my head is killing me, Kaydoos, I hope it isn't the Big C. Oh that pain in my gut. It might be the Big C." He'd gingerly lay a hand on the affected body part, big left palm resting on his forehead and soothing the brain tumor, right hand stroking his flank above the diverticula inflamed from a dinner of brats and spaetzel dotted with rye. "You never know when it will strike. We're all just ticking time bombs."

I didn't know how to give my father any mercy—by which I mean listen to his fears or feel any empathy for his physical and emotional pain. I refused to coddle or cuddle him. All I could do was hold onto the idea that he wanted this, called it in every time he joked about a headache being cancer. I know what he thought. He thought cancer would rally us around him and we'd ply him with enough attention and love to make him whole. He wanted his "girls" around him, rubbing his bald head, scratching his back through his thin, white t-shirt, fixing him bratwurst and sweet rolls for breakfast.

Thanksgiving morning, I went to retrieve them from the hotel and bring them to my house, then part way there I stopped to pick up a new tablecloth. Forty-four years of watching them both—her last minute hairspray and lipstick, his final trip to the bathroom and fumble for the ever missing wallet—I figured I had time.

But it took longer than anticipated. I dithered, unable to decide between the geometric burnt umber and yellow or the fall leaf pattern. When I finally pushed through the Heathman revolving door, I was much later than I should have been. Fifteen minutes? Twenty? Half an hour? I can't remember. The lobby pulsed with human traffic, people racing from the elevators to the dining room, shooting in and out of the revolving doors as if it were a central London roundabout. There, in the middle of the madness, my parents sat side-by-side, looking expectantly. In that moment, they both pierced my heart as if I were seeing them clearly for the first time: two little, round, grey-headed people, looking old and slightly vulnerable, worried they'd gotten their signals crossed and missed their daughter. They both had their coats on even though the lobby was warm. I can't remember what my mother wore, but I remember that my father had on a khaki poplin jacket, zipped halfway. In a trick of memory, I see him wearing the dapper Irish walking cap that he did not buy from the store next door.

THINGS YOU SHOULDN'T TOUCH

A stove element pulsing red.

A woman's belly, swollen with promise, as you ask her when she's due.

Strange dogs—little or big—you never know if they might bite, long incisors sinking into soft flesh.

The medical monitors in an ICU room, no matter how incessantly they beep. Pressing the wrong button causes a team of nurses to stampede into the room behind a bucking crash cart.

The crystal on display at Macy's. *You bull-in-a-china-shop, do you want to wait in the car?*

The thorns on the yellow tea roses arranged in the cut glass vase; but if you can't resist pushing the sharp tips into the fleshy part of your fingers, repeat the following phrase ad nauseum: the only rose without a thorn is love.

Your mother's hair, back-combed and sprayed perfectly into place, even though nothing else is perfect.

Yourself. You'll go blind. You'll grow hair on your palms. You'll get addicted. It will make your wife feel guilty.

BOOGIE NIGHTS

After I first left her, Judy took a few salsa lessons at the Viscount Ballroom where we'd tried to tango together 10 years earlier. Now, ironically, I live just a block away. On summer Saturday nights, they open the huge windows, tipping them out over the street, and the Latin rhythms—drums and horns—and the sound of the instructor calling out steps for salsa and merengue drift out. When I hear the music begin, I lie in the dark, a sweating glass of gin and tonic on the nightstand, and imagine her swinging her hips, head tipped slightly, the small of her back damp under somebody else's palm.

I'm not exactly jealous. I don't want to salsa with her at the Viscount. Still, I can't bear the thought of someone

else touching her. My wife. I mean, my ex-wife. Still somehow mine. Can't bear the thought of someone else—let's
tell the truth—some man, pressing himself against her.
I don't want to think about her submitting to his lead.
I don't want to think about what this means for me and
our 23 years of marriage and all the reasons why we never
danced well together. The few times during our marriage
that anyone turned Judy's head, it was a man. So I have the
feeling that even if I had taken dance lessons and stayed
another 23 years, I probably still would not have danced
well with my wife. Thinking of her dancing with a man
over at the Viscount feels like losing in the worst, most
public way.

⚔

During our 23 year marriage, Judy and I rarely danced
together. This despite beginning our relationship in the
early 80s during the heyday of pop music and fabulous
gay and lesbian dance clubs. The best lesbian bar we ever
went to was the Primary Domain in Portland, Oregon. It
was better than Amelia's in the Mission or Maud's in the
Haight, or the Eastlake East in Seattle (although a high
school prom would have probably been better than the
Eastlake with its filthy bathrooms missing the stall doors,
watered down well drinks, and braless feminist contingent
who insisted on wearing black t-shirts adorned with pho-
to-realistic vulvas).

The bar at the Primary Domain was all Patrick-Nagel-LA-like, full of blonde wood booths, purple carpeting, and pink neon running around the ceiling. You could sit in the bar and actually carry on a conversation—no shouting over the pulsing beat—or make your way to another room where there was a big dance floor, or head off to the well-lit back room with pool tables and pinball machines. The DJs spun vinyl albums ranging from lesbian classics like Joan Armatrading's "Down to Zero" to great pop like "I Can't Wait" by Nu Shooz or "Sweet Dreams" by the Eurythmics. A mix of fast and slow, pop and not, it was the perfect place to dance.

Except we didn't.

I couldn't seem to find the beat or move in any way not resembling a spastic white man. Judy danced in her own world, eyes glazed over, letting the music and movement take her into some ecstatic state that I couldn't reach. It seemed that she rarely even noticed I was with her on the dance floor, compounding the dorkiness I felt. Occasionally, the DJ played a country swing song, and those times, I tried to take Judy's hand and lead. But inevitably that failed to work out, too. I'd miss a beat or step on her foot, or fling her out too hard or too fast, spinning her like an out-of-control top into another couple. Else, she'd tire of the one move I could manage which was pushing her backwards (I got to step forward, a move my mother tells me I mastered at 11 months), and we'd sit back down. Each time, I vowed to sign up for dance lessons. But secretly, I didn't believe they could help us. In college, I'd learned that in his novels, D.H. Lawrence used dancing as a metaphor for sex. If a couple danced well together, it portended nights of great passion. Judy and I seemed to prove Lawrence's theory correct—which is why I didn't really think the lessons would help.

But this is not entirely true. One time we took an Argentinean Tango class with a bunch of straight people. We wanted to support the teacher, our friend Laurie Ann, so we showed up on a Monday night, me in my smooth-soled cowboy boots and Judy in her slick Josef Seibels. It wasn't so bad being the only gay couple in the class; by this time we were well-practiced at being token lesbians. The real discomfort came when Laurie Ann instructed the class to change partners. Judy, who was learning to follow, stepped to her left and into the arms of a waiting man. I closed my eyes, inhaled, and felt sweat break out on my upper lip. When I looked again, a middle-aged white woman stood before me, a tight little half-smile on her lips.

I took a deep breath, trying to push down the shame I suddenly felt. Shame at being butch and leading. Shame because I couldn't move more gracefully. I said, "You don't have to do this. We can wait this out if you want."

This was 1998 or 1999—late enough that this woman didn't want to be seen as homophobic—so instead of bowing out, she simply nodded and took my left hand. I gingerly placed my right on her waist and proceeded to plod her around the room.

The Argentinean Tango is complex, your feet moving backward, forward, and side-to-side while your upper body stays relatively still. The upper body business I could manage, frozen as I was. I looked like a convulsing Tin Man, legs going the wrong way, taking off without letting the rest of me know, torso unyielding. Each time I stepped on my dance partner, or moved backwards when I should have glided forward, cut left when clearly we were supposed to slide right, I apologized, grimaced, swore under my breath. Finally, I let go of her hand and said, "I'm sorry, I'm just no good at this." Right then, Laurie Ann called for us to switch partners again. I looked to Judy to return. But Judy was following the rules. She moved left instead of back towards me and my torture began anew.

This time I danced with a woman who whispered the steps into my right ear and suddenly we began to move together somewhat on time and with a bit of grace. I felt elated. Maybe I just needed more practice. Maybe I could dance, after all. At the next change, Judy returned to me.

"How was it?" I asked.

"That last guy was great. He led me perfectly, barely touching me but still letting me know where he wanted me to go. Ow!"

I'd stepped on her foot.

"You need to relax," she said. "I can't tell what you want me to do, how you want me to move."

"Well, it's a little hard for me to relax when I don't know the steps or, apparently, how to lead."

We slid back-and-forth across the highly varnished wooden floor a few more times and, when I wasn't thinking about where to place my feet, I looked around both levels of the big ball room, searching for a bar. Surely, lubricating myself with a quick martini could help me relax a bit, feel the music. But, alas, no bar. So, instead, I sat and watched as other men danced my wife around the room and she enjoyed it.

Still, there were other times when I would insist on trying to lead. But the only way I knew to do this was to hold Judy closely, my right leg snug between her legs. Thusly positioned, I could push her around the room—more or less—like a Swiffer. Each time I did this it was as if I was saying to both of us: *This is my body, see it.* I could not, would not force Judy into the bedroom, but I was adamant about trying to dance close. I didn't really even like to dance. But when we were at a wedding, a Pink Martini concert, or the damn Viscount Ballroom, I *wanted* to try to dance close to my wife, to approximate the physical relationship we so rarely had. To claim her.

But it is hard to dance when you are not totally inhabiting your body and, during this time, I tried not to think about my body much. So when I see a picture taken during these years I think, *who is that woman with the thick neck, the picnic hams for upper arms, the flotation device around her midsection?* In my imagination, I was more butch and attractive: stocky not obese, muscled not massive, strong not slothful. And while it is certainly true that any person can learn to move gracefully, I did not. Was it because I simply weighed too much to shimmy and glide, or was it because both people in the marriage ignored my body? Maybe the why is unimportant. Maybe what's important is the dissonance I felt between how I wanted it to be and the reality.

⇒⇒ ⇐⇐

I have a picture of the very last time Judy and I danced together. I call it *Portrait of a Marriage Dissolving* and I keep the photo tucked in a desk drawer that I don't open very often.

The photo was shot at a friend's wedding in North Carolina, just a week before I moved out of the house. I initially ordered a print of it because I liked that we were dressed up and that she was in my arms. And, truth be told, I thought we wouldn't really divorce. I imagined that I would take some time away and realize that—whatever our troubles—I'd rather face them with her than alone. I wanted to have this picture so that ten years later, we could look at it and know that although we'd been falling apart that night, although Judy went to bed twenty minutes after that picture was taken and cried for two solid hours while I lay in the dark next to her saying, "I'm sorry, I'm sorry, I'm sorry," that although this had happened, we'd survived our crucible.

Of course all I have now is a picture. It pains me to look at it and remember that night and how I tried to connect with Judy on the dance floor, as if by acting chivalrous and graceful, holding her close in the circle of us, I could push back the previous two months. It had happened so suddenly. It seemed as if we were sliding across the dance floor of our life together, gracefully dipping and turning, a couple who'd danced together for more than 20 years. Then, in a matter of moments, we were on the sidelines, the heel snapped off one of my shoes and a cramp in my calf. Of course, it had started much earlier, my shoe wearing unevenly as we tried to match our gait to each other, our muscles fatiguing from stepping repeatedly around dance floor obstacles we both tried hard to ignore.

But that night I thought that if I could try again, just get the steps right, I could save our marriage.

"Not now," she said, when I asked her and, "Let's wait until the dance floor is less crowded." Or, "It's too hot in there." I think Etta James' song "At Last" was playing when Judy finally stepped with me onto the parquet floor, she in her brown linen skirt and the shirt she'd worn to our own wedding three years earlier. I'm sure she sighed, sounding resigned and exhausted at the same time. It was close to 11:00 p.m. and we'd been going steady in the North Carolina heat and humidity since 7:00 a.m., drinking since noon when I'd poured the first batch of Bombay Sapphire gin and tonics. So, she probably did feel exhausted, but her sigh spoke volumes, coming after I'd pestered her to dance, just as the singer was crescendoing, *At last, at last, at last, the skies above are blue.* If I were writing a movie script,

I'd put that sigh right there and every person would know by the sound of it that the story wasn't going to have a happy ending.

I remember her stiff in my arms and pulling back just a bit so that our breasts still touched, but not our bellies or thighs. I remember stepping out, my arms taut and bent only partially, to twirl her under my left arm. I remember this failing because she hijacked the lead. In my memory and the photo, our faces shine with perspiration. It was 80 degrees with humidity to match even though the sun had set five hours earlier. Everyone at the reception was dripping, including the natives. Yet, even then, I recognized the acrid tang of fear in my own sweat, fear that I couldn't pull this one off. When I look at that picture now, I can still recall that sharp scent and not the smell of Judy's perfume.

Judy looks frozen. Or maybe that is just my projection. But I don't think so. The hands tell otherwise. Her delicate right hand, with its thin bird bones, is closed over my left thumb, while the rest of my big paw covers the back of her hand and appears to be clamped over her wrist and part of her forearm, as well, as if I am trying to keep her under control. Or from bolting.

"I didn't want to be in that room with all those people, I remember that much," she tells me when I ask her about that night, about the picture.

"Because we were the only gay people and you felt conspicuous, the South and all?"

"I felt conspicuous for sure, but mostly because I was falling apart. I just wanted to be alone with you. I felt like you were a lifeboat that I was clinging to. I was just hanging on so tightly."

On my left arm, the one gripping Judy, I am wearing a malachite bracelet that I bought 14 years earlier in Mexico, where I had gone to think the first time our marriage seemed truly in jeopardy. And I am wearing my wedding ring. Not the first one, the gold band we bought at JC Penney's: I lost that one somewhere in the Beaverton Mall. Not the second one, custom made with all the diamonds and sapphires: I lost 30 pounds and that one no longer fit. I am wearing the third ring: a wide, woven silver band that I picked out alone at Tiffany's. When I look at this photo, that ring and the way I am gripping Judy is what first catches my gaze, I suppose because I don't wear a ring anymore and, even a year later, I still sometimes feel it there and am surprised to look down and find my finger bare.

I stand in the foreground as if I am about to burst out of the dance, out of our life, and the photographer's flash catches me more than Judy. I am illuminated and she, while not exactly in shadow, does not seem to glow as brightly. She stands with her body slightly behind center, our right hips almost even. Looking at this picture now, I realize I had danced us, quite literally, into a corner and we couldn't get out until the photographer had finished his work. I don't remember, but I'd guess that our dance ended after the photographer snapped the picture that captured the end of our marriage.

Before heading off to bed though, Judy suffered through one more dance. The bride's father grabbed Judy and pulled her into a swing dance.

She told me later, "I kept telling him no, telling him he didn't understand, that I was in the middle of a serious conversation. But he insisted."

I didn't see this happen or else I'd have cut in one last time.

SIR MA'AM SIR: GENDER FRAGMENTS

I was 9 the first time I was mistaken for a boy. I stood in the candy aisle of Long's Drugs store, trying to decide between a Big Hunk, a Charleston Chew, or Milk Duds. It was winter, I know that much, and I wore a blue quilted coat with a white faux fur-trimmed hood. I hated that hood, but my mother was adamant about girly clothes. She didn't want me mistaken for a boy.

The clerk thought I was stealing, I'm sure, lurking as I was amongst the chocolate and caramel. He stuck his head around the end-cap and said, "What do you have in your pocket there, son?"

My heart started pounding and I blushed hard, skin showing each and every emotion that crossed my heart. I didn't look up. "Nothing."

"Go on, now, and be a good boy and show me what you have there."

I pulled my hands out, bringing the contents of both left and right pockets with me. It wasn't unusual for me to have my father's boyhood pocket knife, the one he'd given me against—I imagine—the admonition of my mother, I am sure. This day, though, my pockets were surprisingly "girl." In my left hand I held a watermelon-flavored Bonnie Bell Lip Smacker, in the right a wadded up Kleenex and a dollar bill. I may have also produced a Wonder Woman Pez dispenser. Nine was the year of the Pez. I looked the clerk squarely in the face, barely controlling my tears, palms turned up.

"Ah, um, all right, then. Go on, now, sweetie."

In the late 70s, gaucho skirts—the precursor to skorts— were popular. My mom took me to Sears and urged me to try on a denim one.

The sales lady even chimed in. "It's the look of a skirt but with the freedom of pants."

That was the problem. It had the look of a skirt. While I didn't want to be mistaken for a boy, neither did I want to have to dress like a girl.

━━ ━━

I can't remember if the lapels of the tuxedo jacket were crushed velvet or shiny satin, some of the details are simply lost to the degrading dendrites and failing synapses of time. It was a black jacket, however, even though it was 1982 and it could have easily been powder blue. The shirt was a classic tuxedo shirt, the buttons and bow tie permanently attached. You actually slid into the shirt back to front and secured it up the back with a bit of Velcro, the quicker to get the high school seniors in and out of the photo studio.

Still. Tuxedo.

This is how it felt to change from the black velvet drape to the tuxedo: it was like diving into a cool, mineral-laden river, the way water slides all silky over skin turned pink from too much July sun, the way a body moves with the current—slipping along seemingly languidly only to find itself much further downstream than expected.

Or it felt like this: like a sigh made at the end of a long day when at last you can crawl into your big, king-sized bed just made with clean, purple 600-thread count Egyptian cotton sheets—like a whisper across your tired body—the memory foam mattress a reminder of what soft is supposed to feel like.

It did not feel like sitting exposed on top of a white rock mesa in New Mexico's Chaco Canyon, the wind kicking up the fine grit of desert topsoil and the pulverized sandstone, exfoliating the fair Irish skin on my cheeks and neck, searing my eyes, worrying my chattering mind about melanomas and carcinomas and survival in this too-bright landscape. No, that's what the velvet drape—off the shoulder, no pushup bra or pearls—felt like.

The way I remember it is that it didn't occur to me NOT to wear a tuxedo for my senior portrait. I felt handsome not beautiful, dapper not sexy. Of course tuxedo rather than drape. Of course bow tie rather than earrings.

Then the proofs arrived in the mail.

Although I can't remember whether the lapels of the jacket were soft or silky under my fingertips, I remember what my mother said when she got to the last three pictures in the stack of proofs, after all the various poses with the drape—looking left, looking right, looking back over my shoulder—when she got to the last three photos her voice rose half an octave, grew loud, and she said, "What in the world were you thinking?"

Good question, that.

For someone who was forbidden to wear her favored 501s and plaid flannel to school presumably because they accentuated the butch in her, someone who only allowed herself the most cursory of thoughts about what these clothes signified, someone who stood mute, scuffing a toe nervously back and forth across the sidewalk any time Alison Green stood too close in all her Love's Baby Soft glory, what was I thinking? How did that kid find the courage to ask the photographer if he—and the photographer was a he—to ask if he would take her picture in a tuxedo? Did she find it easier to make the request with his head tucked under the black fabric that hung off the box camera? Like the safety of the confessional her father entered on Saturdays, was it somehow easier to say to a face she could not see, *Forgive me Father for I have sinned. It has been six weeks since I last wanted to wear a tuxedo. And Lord, I want to wear one today and be memorialized in color.*

"Sir, I'll need you to step over here so I can check your bag." Some minimum wage earning man in a wrinkled white shirt with a TSA shoulder patch indicates I should follow him.

"I beg your pardon?"

"Sir, I'll need you . . ."

I interrupt him by clearing my throat and look him dead in the eyes. " . . . What is it you need?"

"Sir. Ma'am I'll need you to . . ."

" . . . fine."

I am always surly, a mixture of annoyance tinged with a hint of shame. I pull on my coat, straighten my cuffs and collar and stare straight ahead while the TSA drone searches my bag.

"Looks like everything is okay here." They always try to sound perky after calling me sir.

If I fly coach instead of first class, the confusion continues. The cabin crew rushes to serve people as quickly as possible. They glance down, see grey streaking back from the temples and look no further. They don't look at skin or jewelry. Perhaps they scan clothing, admittedly slightly androgynous, dark shirt and jeans, or deep red shirt with French cuffs and pinstriped pants purchased—ironically—in the women's department at Nordstrom.

"Something to drink for you, sir?"

Again, I clear my throat. "Yes, I'd like . . ."

". . . Ma'am. Oh my, gosh, I'm sorry, ma'am. What would you like?"

⇒⊹ ⊹⇐

I'm waiting for the TSA agent at San Francisco International Airport. He looks up, says "Sir," and motions me forward.

I smile, don't correct him, hand him my driver's license.

"Kathleen?"

"Yes."

"Please wait over there." He points to a spot behind his dais and then calls for a higher authority. Apparently, there was more question in *Kathleen* than simple confirmation of my name.

He hangs onto my driver's license and I wait, watch others whisk a step closer to their full body scans. My girlfriend won the TSA Pre-Check lottery and I can barely see her petite frame resplendent in a sun dress and the

65

turquoise sandals she was allowed to leave on. She waits on the other side of the security bottleneck. I imagine her scanning the crowd, looking expectantly for my grey hair and tortoise shell glasses. This is the first time we have flown together and I've warned her that the TSA agents are flustered by lack of gender conformity.

I wait for 11 minutes. Finally, a big, bleached blonde African American lady huffs up to the Asian TSA agent. The three of us, we could hold a mini social justice meet-up right here if we wanted. But that's not how this goes.

"What's the problem here?" She juts her chin towards him.

The man hands his superior my driver's license and says, "His name is Kathleen."

The woman looks at the license. Looks at me. Looks at her subordinate. "Are you kidding me?" She shouts this at the agent. Then she thrusts my license at me and says, "Come on! I'm showing you to the front of the line. You've waited long enough."

She glares back at the male agent with all the haughty imperiousness that only a big black lady can manage, and I'm secretly pleased at the trouble I suspect he is in.

My beloved sees me and my escort now, then watches as another female agent frisks me after I have walked through the metal detector. I look over at my girlfriend, my eyes hooded, my face as impassive as I can manage as the agent runs her hands up and down my legs, across my arms spread wide, along my spine and flanks, around my waist. Finally, she asks if she can lift my untucked shirt and examine my belt. I nod, and as the agent pulls up the red linen and puts her nitrile gloved hand on my belt, I watch my girlfriend's mouth drop open and I worry she is going to start getting uppity. Our eyes meet and I shake my head slightly. She closes her mouth, looks towards the floor, and waits for me to join her.

We see gender because it's what we are conditioned to see. The notion that gender rests on a continuum just as sexuality does seems to unnerve people so much that they forget about the complexities and differences in their own lives and the lives of those they know. The man who likes to sew and cries each time he watches *On Golden Pond*. The woman who can run a skill saw and a drill press and still loves her Bare Minerals makeup. It is not an innate ability to nurture children and want missionary style sex that makes a woman female any more than being the provider for the family and watching NASCAR makes men male. If you think about it in these terms, everyone is trying to transcend gender and gender roles.

Well, then what are you? Declare yourself, we cry—or at least that TSA agent did. Twenty years ago, I would have called myself an androgyne, from the Greek aner, meaning man, and gyne, meaning woman. It used to mean the mixing of masculine and feminine characteristics—at least in terms of fashion—or a balance of anima and animus in Jungian psychoanalytical theory. In terms of gender identity, it has come to mean a person who does not fit easily into the typical masculine or feminine gender roles of their society. For me, androgyne seemed softer than butch. Butch scared me, or, more accurately, butch shamed me.

Twenty years ago, positive images of butch women were hidden, if they existed at all. The gay and lesbian communities thought butches were perpetuating heterosexist norms and that our masculinity jeopardized the "we're just like you" image that many organizations promoted as a way to hasten acceptance. The mainstream culture—well, how do I know what was running through their collective heads? Men's treatment of me lead me to believe that they thought my swagger meant I wanted their wives, my dress meant I wished I were male (Thank you, Dr. Freud). Some women thought it was their job to school me, making overt comments about a "little makeup" and "softer" clothes (whether they meant angora or more gender-specific, I never inquired).

For a while, I dated a young genderqueer ten years my junior who was at turns both beautiful and handsome. She had great "gay credibility," a trait my friends demanded I search for. The GQ's credibility stemmed from her founding of Portland's Sexual Minority Youth Resource Center (SMYRC). SMYRC provided a refuge for kids questioning their sexual orientation, gender, or gender presentation. It was a place where no one did a double take at a girl in a bow tie or a boy in a dress, a sort of Boys and Girls Club for queers, a levee against the rising depression and despair so many queer kids face.

The original locations stood only about three blocks from the apartment I moved to after I left Judy—a neighborhood for the divorced and dispossessed, where coffee shops and pool halls butted up against pre-war apartment buildings and the Sons of Norway meeting hall sat next to a hipster hair salon. All of this is jammed into 10-square blocks bordered by the Willamette River on one side and Sandy Boulevard on the other. The innermost inner city.

The GQ told me that tough butches manned the door at SMYRC, ensuring that homeless drunks and domineering homophobes didn't wander in to the Friday night drag shows or Saturday night movies. One night, a drunk man approached Sarah, a petite 5'2" bouncer. The man could see a pool table inside and he tried pushing his way into the former tattoo parlor. But Sarah firmly rebuffed the man.

The drunk eyed her, confused by her resolve.

"Hey, what are you?" he demanded.

Sarah didn't answer, instead insisting the man along.

Half a block later, he turned around and shouted back to Sarah, "Hey, I know what you are! You're a lady man!"

The GQ laughed and laughed and laughed when she told me this story. Her delight at being part of a cadre that confused the cultural mainstream loosened some shame that I had always carried. Before the GQ, here is what I heard each time someone called me sir: *Gee you are an ugly woman.* But the GQ chose me because I am butch. The GQ liked that I confused and flustered store clerks. And I liked that the GQ liked this—and me—and so I started to like myself a little bit more.

The hottest thing a woman ever did was to tug on the waistband of my jeans and say, "Got a little something in there for me?" In that moment the last of my shame and confusion fell away. This woman wanted me *because* I was butch. As much as she wanted the jeans and the boots, the ties and the snap-on-tools, she also wanted the energy— my yang to her yin, my butch to her femme. Maybe that's at the heart of it for me, this energetic play back and forth. It's a dance I've always been able to do, even when I professed not to know the steps.

THE LAST TIME EVERYTHING WAS NORMAL

Who knows when it was? Seven years have passed and I've stopped living the story, stopped retelling it to my new girlfriends. I think now, I just hang onto the moments that seemed normal and yet numinous. Like walking down Yamhill Street in March 2007 when the ornamental cherry trees were in full bloom, their double pink blossoms like an explosion of fecundity. We were holding hands and ambling back towards our house where my sick mother lay sleeping. She shouldn't have been there, but she was because we were so very good at keeping things alive—ill parents, weak cats, leggy plants, our marriage.

Another time, 2004, Mallorca. We'd been traveling together for three weeks and then had spent several days apart—me at a writers' retreat, you on a Mediterranean beach with Kate Rushton. A foreign language, a Catalan dialect, buses and hotel negotiations all without the sturdy familiarity of each other. We'd pre-arranged to meet midway through my retreat, just for a couple of hours. When you saw me lumbering up the cobblestone hill, you ran down to me, buried your face in my neck and cried. Once recovered, you said, "You promised to always talk for me in foreign countries!" A joke between us because while I retained the vocabulary, your tongue rolled impeccably over the double Rs and lisping esses of Spain. Too soon, I had to return to the writing colony.

Or, 1997, when we finally finished remodeling the original kitchen in our 1910 Edwardian. We'd taken it down to the studs ourselves. The new maple cabinets and Pergo floors made the room deluxe. Stainless steel replaced harvest gold and a 4x4 window shone light through what had been a solid wall. We stood there satisfied that the vision we'd imagined 8 years earlier had come to fruition. You turned to me and said, "I hope the adults who live here don't get mad when they find us in their kitchen."

Or maybe it was July 2007. We were sitting at the teak table outside our yurt, on the 20 acres we'd purchased 9 years earlier. You wore a purple rugby-striped tank top. Do you remember it? I remember finding you so authentically beautiful with your hair piled loose on your head, your sunglasses pushed up to the edge of your hairline. "Here, let me take your picture and show you what I see," I said. As I remember it, you shrugged when I showed you the picture.

I still have it. The smartphone craze was only beginning and this was the first of a digital locker's-worth of photos. When I look at it now, that transcendence I remember feeling is missing. In its place is a memory of the stillness of that day with you, and the pain of losing it all too quickly.

YELLOW SORROW

Cardiac Cath Lab, St. Joseph's Hospital, Tacoma, Washington.

It's dead quiet in here: no television blaring CNN or Dr. Phil or NASCAR. I've been sitting here for an hour, waiting for my mother. A typical angiogram takes about one hour, an hour-and-a-half if the cardiologist can place a stent in the offending artery. As the minutes march on— 65, 75, 85, 95, 100—I feel my gut clamp down and taste metal. I want to get up and run out of here and keep running until I collapse from pain in my own chest.

The nurse who prepped my mother—shaved her pubic hair, washed her groin with Betadine—pokes her head out. My neck and face flush.

"You're still here?"

I nod.

"Mary, right?" She says my mother's name.

I nod again.

"Let me get the doctor."

The cardiologist comes out in scrubs. He says, "Let's step in here."

I think: stay present. Do not panic. Do not cry.

"Let me show you your mom's heart," he says and points to a computer screen.

I do not like this man. His nose is red and veined like an alcoholic's, his skin is sallow. He talks too fast. On the monitor is an image of my mother's heart with five blocked arteries, including a 90% occlusion in the left anterior descending artery, the artery the cardiologists call the widow-maker.

My lip quivers, for just a moment, when he says, "The only chance your mother has is with an emergency bypass surgery right now. We've called a surgeon and we've got to start the paperwork immediately."

I stop him, ask him to draw out the occlusions so I can relay the information to my father who is not here, to my sisters who live in San Francisco, to my wife in Portland. I must not be the only one who has ever made this request because he grabs a piece of paper with a drawing of a heart and its arteries and hastily sketches out the blockages, writes down the artery names. Then the surgery coordinator blows into the room, all caffeine and efficiency, and begins talking loud and fast. Or maybe none of these people are talking fast. Maybe everything has just slowed down for me. Maybe the time for hushed tones is over.

⟞⟝

The surgery coordinator and I run down a brightly lit hallway in the cath lab, trying to catch up with my mother's gurney. We run alongside it just as if we were in some TV show.

"We'll do a Doppler of her leg veins, map them out and see if they're good. Surgery takes four or five hours, typically. Four or five days in the hospital and then we'll see about rehab. I hate to ask, but what type of insurance?"

"Medicare, supplemental through AARP." I hope this is the right answer.

"Oh, that's great. You'll be fine then. I've got to get things moving. One of the surgeons will be up to talk to you soon." She peels off, still running, down another long hallway.

I'm left with two orderlies and my mother. She is still drugged from the angiogram, in and out of consciousness. I touch her arm. It's fleshy and clammy, how a dead person pumped full of formaldehyde must feel—I push the thought from my head.

"Hi, Honey." My mom smiles all groggy.

"Mom, you're going to need a bypass."

"Really?"

"Yes, five arteries."

"Are you sure? I was convinced I'd just need a stent." She closes her eyes and drifts off.

We get back to her room and I call each of my sisters, explain what's happening, give the phone to my drugged mother. Each time she says the same thing: "Oh, Honey, don't cry. I'm going to be fine, fine. I'll feel so much better when this is done. We're going to take trips together, maybe a cruise."

I call my father. "They're prepping her for emergency bypass," I say right after he says "hello."

"I'm on my way," he says in a sing-songy voice. As if he is merely running late to a meeting.

"She'll be in surgery by the time you get here. Do you want to talk to her?"

"Put her on," he says.

⇒⊢ ⊣⇐

Last night, when I was at yoga, he left a voice message telling me my mother had suffered a heart attack and was being transported off the Olympic Peninsula to St. Joseph's Hospital in Tacoma, two hours away. I called him back and said, "I'll meet you there. I'm just packing and I'll be on the road in ten minutes."

"I'm not going. They're just taking her to the cath lab to look at the blockages."

"What?"

77

"Your mother told me I didn't have to go. Jesus, it's late, Kaydoos, and besides, who would watch the dogs. I can't leave them alone here. Did you hear me? They're only looking for blockages. I'll come in the morning, after my dentist appointment."

I'm not sure what part of for better or worse he fails to understand, exactly why he chafes against his caretaking responsibility. I suppose there is no easy answer to the question of why my father is not here. Partly he is not here because he is very concrete and truly believed my mother when she told him he didn't need to come to Tacoma. Partly, he is anxiety-ridden. Unable to cope with a spontaneous change in plans. He really does worry that his dogs will suffer if he leaves them alone—even though his neighbor runs a kennel and will care for them. Partly, his processing capabilities are slow enough that he is unable to cope with a spontaneous change in plans and inflexible enough that he often can't see other options. And partly he is a prime-grade narcissist who doesn't want his routine disturbed.

He does come to the hospital the night she is having bypass surgery. He shows up an hour after the surgery has begun, stays long enough to bond with a "poor veteran waiting all alone" for a neighbor who is in surgery. He fails to see the parallel of his daughter—alone—waiting for her mother, his wife, to come out of surgery and, instead, heads home after only 3 hours in the waiting room, leaving me to wait another 6 hours.

━═‹╞ ‹╞━

I am alone again in the surgery waiting room. At 9:35 pm the phone rings. The call can be for no one except me.

"Hello, this is Kate."

"Kate, this is Jackie, Dr. Smith's scrub nurse. How you doin'?" Her Southern drawl languid, as if there were no emergency bypass surgery in progress.

"How's my mom?"

"She's doin' well. We've got the veins harvested. Took a little longer than expected but everything's okay. We're goin' to put your mom on bypass at about 9:45, is that okay with you?"

"Sure." What else am I going to say?

"I'll call you in an hour, but don't you worry, your mom's doin' great."

I start crying before I replace the receiver. Great big gasps that I make no attempt to contain. My cell phone rings, I'm ten minutes late with the update calls, the fifth one of the evening. I somehow cease all crying and turn once again—or maybe it is for the first time—into the matriarch of my family. I give my sisters Sue and Jule the update first, then call my wife, Judy. I try to reassure everyone, sound like I'm not worried. They try to support me the best they can from 250 and 900 miles away, but, really, what can they say?

Finally, I call my father who left an hour earlier.

"I missed the ferry," he says. "I'm just sitting here waiting for the next one. It's going to be midnight before I get home."

I hang up, listen to the blood pounding in my ears. Breathe. Finally, the hum of the florescent lights overrides the heartbeat of rage.

9:45 p. m. I shiver with an almost unbearable cold and sob into my backpack. I've carried it all day—along with my laptop—believing I'd work during the angiogram. All I can think is that my mom is clinically dead right now and I feel too young to lose her. I don't want her to die under the harsh light of the OR. I don't want her to be cold. They lowered her body temperature to 88 degrees in order to put her on the heart-lung machine.

I pant, catch my breath in that way you do when big grief overtakes you.

The door opens and I look up, make no attempt to wipe away the snot coursing down my face.

"Long night, huh?" a woman in scrubs asks me.

I nod.

"I'm an OR nurse."

Oh. That's why I can't stop crying. Intuitively, I must have known she was dead.

The nurse raises her hand in a stop gesture, as if she knows I am beginning to spin out of control. "Your mom's doing great, but you look like you might need a cup of coffee. Are you here by yourself?"

I nod yes to both.

"Cream?"

"Whatever. I'll take whatever."

I hold tightly to the paper cup she brings me, my hand covering the playing cards printed at jaunty angles. If I were in my right mind, I would comment on the ironic use of printing a straight flush on a cup of vending machine coffee. Instead, I suck it down, all bitter tasting and full of preservative-laden non-dairy creamer. I don't know that I've ever tasted a finer cup. I start crying again. The coffee, the kind gesture, my cold, cold mother.

"Do you have siblings?"

"Two sisters. San Francisco." I balance the coffee cup on the seat cushion and blow my nose. "I'm sorry."

"You don't have to apologize. Is your mom married?"

I take a deep breath. For the first of many times I am asked to explain my father's absence. But that is not exactly true. People simply ask if my mother is married and it is I who feel some compunction to explain why her husband is missing from this vigil.

"He was here, but he's gone home now," I tell Karen. Her name is Karen and she's training to be a scrub nurse.

Her eyebrows rise just slightly, but she catches herself. Now it is her turn to nod and then she reaches across the couch and takes my hand.

I realize right then that the simplest answer is the most stunning: he was here but he left.

Before he left, he gave me the name of the mortuary he'd like me to use. "Just in case, Kaydoos. You know, in case the worst should happen."

⤚⤙ ⤚⤙

At 1:45 a.m. the surgeon finally enters the surgery waiting room, still empty except for me. I've turned off most of the lights and pace in the glow of the Food Network. The television has broadcast for ten hours, oblivious to my waiting room drama, through news and sitcoms, reality shows and late night news shows. Food Network, Discovery Channel, Comedy Central, TV Land: normally I'd sate myself, but the sound, the color, and quick camera angles jar me. I keep the television on for background noise only, a low murmur to remind me that life really does exist outside of the liminal space of the surgery waiting room.

"So, your mom did okay."

Wendell Smith, the cardiac surgeon, peers at me from baggy, bloodshot eyes. His scrubs are not spattered with blood which I take as a good omen, failing to realize he likely changed before coming out to see me. Around his neck is a pair of binocular magnifying glasses that say 25x on the side. I can't let myself think about him staring intently through them as he uses silk thread to sew my mother's just harvested mammary artery to her heart, bypassing the left anterior descending artery which was 90% occluded.

"Took awhile," I have no idea what else to say to him. I think that the worst must be over. She survived the surgery even though it took 11 hours instead of 4 or 5.

"Your mom arrested during the surgery and once before."

I stare at him.

Smith continues, "She's all right. The next twenty-four, forty-eight hours are crucial, though."

Oh. Of course. She's more than 100 pounds over-weight, she smoked for 52 years, she just underwent quin-tuple bypass. Still, I calm myself, my dad was even more overweight and the VA released him only five days after his bypass. I think of the four days of clothes that I packed, think it should be enough if I go commando one day and don't pit out my shirts.

Oh, and if there aren't any med errors, no infection that blows her incision apart, no kidney failure, no conges-tive heart failure, if the pulmonologist can take my moth-er off the ventilator in the morning. If everything goes according to plan.

After the fact, I realize that my father is angry that my moth-er stole his thunder. He had a bypass, too, as he never fails to mention. He pulls open his red plaid shirt to expose the scar where the VA surgeons split his sternum. His head shakes with a palsy he's had for the past 15 years and he breathes through his mouth, his lips slick with saliva. "What do you think of that?" he says. His eyes bug out slightly for emphasis and his breath is heavy. "Two bypasses in one family."

The nurses and doctors nod and continue their life-saving work on my mother. There is no *My gosh! What are the odds?* If his comment even registers at all, it's probably with a thought of *That's not really surprising*, which is something they cannot say out loud.

It is this lack of attention that hurts his chest more than any heart attack, more than any bypass surgery. I watch him quietly button his shirt back up and mumble to himself, "Yeah, well. I'm in cardiac rehab, now."

⇒⊦ ⊣⇐

I am the girl who always hated going to the butcher. I could not bear to see the meat locker open to reveal the slightly swaying sides of beef, pork, lamb. I'd shut my eyes and cover my ears when the butcher pushed a prime rib through the band saw, or cracked a lamb shank with a quick swing of a cleaver.

Now, I stare at a giant gash of meat: 10 inches long, four inches wide, three inches deep. I see sternum. Shiny gold-colored titanium plates hold the sternum together. A thin line reveals where surgeons cut the sternum (not with a band saw, I hope). On the left where the surgeon points, I see pericardium, the sack surrounding the heart, and if I follow the line of the wound up past clavicle and chin, I can look into my mother's eyes.

The wound looks awful, brown and yellow with necrotic fat in some areas, pink and raw like hamburger in others. The sternum itself looks long and yellow. I recall seventh grade geography and a text book line about the

Yangtze that ran the length of China. The Chinese called it "the yellow sorrow."

Twenty years ago, this would have killed my mother or else taken three years to close because the body repairs itself from the inside out, tissue growing up from the deepest point towards the surface. But modern technology has changed wound care as much as antibiotics have changed infections. Now my mother is connected 24-hours-a-day to a machine called a Wound Vac. The Wound Vac speeds healing by creating negative pressure inside the wound. The vacuum sucks out all the serosanguinous fluid and infection that lies in the base, while the negative pressure of the vacuum pulls the tissue tight against a piece of foam that's been placed in the wound. This encourages new cell growth, or granulation. The new cells force out the infected bits and ultimately fill in the wound. Ultimately.

After seven weeks in ICU, I move my mother to a rehab hospital in Oregon. Rehab hospital is really just a nice word for nursing home—a place where people either get better or they die. Which outcome do we want for my mother? Which outcome does she want for herself?

I chaperone her for appointments with doctors: cardiologists, thoracic surgeons, plastic surgeons, infectious disease doctors, endocrinologists. There are X-rays and wound cultures, IV therapy to ensure everything is okay with the PICC line that runs from the brachial artery on my mom's left arm, up through the maze of other arteries, to the vena cava just above her heart. Everyday an hour's worth of antibiotics drips through this line as we try to combat MRSA, MRSE, and a host of other antibiotic-resistant bacteria that infect her chest. Now, exposure to new germs in a new hospital has led to c-diff—also known as the barfing-shitting disease—and e-coli that grows in her wound, and klebsiella pneumonia, each disease treated with yet another antibiotic.

Then there is the changing of the chest dressing, a two hour endeavor my mother endures every other day, plus physical and occupational therapies where she learns to use a wheeled walker and pace herself in the activities of daily living.

"Can you walk to the nurses' station without stopping?" the physical therapist asks my mother. "I think you can if you go slowly enough."

My mother tries never to show her physical or emotional distress. She believes acting "as-if" will somehow make it so. As if she hasn't spent the last ten weeks hospitalized. As if she doesn't need oxygen when she walks. As if standing perfectly erect at the walker and moving more quickly than she should will somehow prove she's not that debilitated and then the physical therapist will leave her alone.

Halfway to the nurses' station, 25 feet from where she started, my mother must lock the brakes on her walker and sit down on its padded seat.

"You moved too quickly. If you slow it down, you can walk 50 feet without stopping."

A tear rolls down my mother's cheek. "I used to be a gymnast."

What happened to my perfectly coiffed mother with her Esteé Lauder makeup, silver hair set and backcombed into place, a choker of Mikimoto pearls lying across her collarbone? What happened to the mother who haunts my dreams: tan, clad in a muslin-colored caftan and gold lamé Capezios, her arms spread wide, gold bracelets pealing, welcoming guests to a dinner party?

By January 19th, my mother has been in two different hospitals for a total of 106 days. Something happens to a person when they've been institutionalized that long, when practically every decision is made for them. On days when we do not need to visit the team of specialists, my mother can choose to get up or not, get dressed or not, eat or not. Everything else is decided either by the nursing staff or me. My mother willingly cedes control to me with relatively few requests. But by the first week in January, she becomes convinced she will die if she does not get out of the hospital and she begs me to bring her home.

My father also pleads with me to bring my mother home. He's lonely. She'll do better at home. The facility I've chosen is no good. He has a different reason every time I talk to him. Neither of them has a clue about the level of care she truly requires. She cannot bathe or dress herself, she cannot change any of her wound dressings, she does not remember to take her medications without prompting, she does not remember to test her blood sugar before meals, or what insulin dose she needs, she cannot cook her meals, or even fix a snack. She often requires oxygen on exertion and breathing treatments with a mask and an albuterol suspension three-times a day. She will need to make a daily trip to the outpatient IV infusion center in Port Angeles. Forty-five minutes each way, plus ninety minutes for the vancomycin to drip through her PICC line. Still, I am dutiful, respectful and manage to move her home. To die, I think, and so do the dogs: they take one sniff and walk away from her.

Moving my mother home is a Herculean effort re-quiring coordination between three different teams of doctors in Washington and Oregon, as well as complying with the various Medicare rules for each state and the ar-cane regulations and policies at the rehab hospital. For two weeks prior to the discharge I carry a clipboard with me everywhere I go because doctors, insurance adjust-ers, discharge planners, and home health nurses call at all hours. Finally, on January 19th, everything seems to be in place and I pack my mother into the Prius along with the Wound Vac and its supplies, additional dressing supplies for her leg wounds, oxygen and various different breathing apparatuses, and thirty-seven 5x7 cards with a Timothy-Leary-worthy all-you-can-eat buffet of drugs sealed onto each card. My mother's name is printed next to the drug name, dosage, and time the medicine should be administered. Card after card purchased with Medicare dollars from the nursing home pharmacy. This system is supposed to idiot-proof the twice daily dispensing of medication within the nursing home. The a.m. cards fill one med cart, the p.m. cards fill another.

When we left, the nursing home gave us all the medications already blister-packed and stored on the med carts. I signed for the controlled substances—oxycontin, oxycodone, xanax, valium, and ativan—a happy meal of addictive substances to keep pain and anxiety at bay. In addition to the "fun" drugs, we also have Cipro, Coreg, Cymbalta, Lasix, Levamir, metronidazole, Novolog, spironolactone, Synthroid, vancomycin, and Zocor. Asmanex and Spiriva, two inhalers to help with COPD (chronic obstructive pulmonary disease, or what your grandmother used to call emphysema) round out the drugs I've pulled from the white plastic bag that says "Marquis Care." I wonder what "Roi Care" looks like.

I sit at the kitchen table, popping pills from their packages and filling my mother's blue pill boxes. I have no idea how my parents are going to manage this once I leave. "Lasix, forty milligrams, bee eye dee," I repeat to myself as I drop the pills. Fourteen times, Monday through Sunday, twice a day, two boxes. "Spironolactone, twelve point five milligrams qew dee," I say. Seven times, Monday through

Sunday, one box. I put the pill into the morning box. It's a diuretic and I don't want my mom up all night making trips to the bathroom.

My father stands behind me and watches. "Let me ask you something, Kaydoos. Is the Cymbalta twice a day now?"

He shatters my rhythm. I think, Cymbalta, twenty milligrams bee eye dee. "Yes, Dad." I can't remember if the pill cards I've yet to use are on my left or right, damn it.

"And the spurn-ee-lactone, it does what?"

"Spur-on-i-lactone. It's a diuretic, Dad. Can you see I'm a little busy here?"

"I'm just trying to understand here, Kaydoos. You've been doing this for four months now. This is my first day."

I take a deep breath and will myself to soften, to have the slightest bit of compassion. "Fair enough, Dad. Anything else you want to know about her meds?"

He sits and lifts the first of 37 cards. "Coreg, that's a heart medication, right? I've seen the commercials."

"Yes, specifically it helps with blood pressure and congestive heart failure."

I try to keep my voice level and calm as I answer his questions, explain the drug regimen and wound care routine, things he would know had he been at the hospital with us.

I didn't know then that five more months of care-giving lay on the horizon. That night it seemed we had sailed through the worst storm. But then I was never very good at getting my bearings, the sextant and compass my Navy father's tools, not my own.

❧ ❧

As I drove my mother home, I asked her how she could stay with my father. "Well, Honey, I think I've chosen not to remember so much because otherwise I couldn't bear it," she said.

But her body remembers, and the anger and despair she purports to forget is literally breaking her heart. In the ICU, after she'd been removed from the ventilator and could finally speak again, she asked me where my father was. A nurse was in the room, checking the various monitors, lines, and IVs.

"He's in Sequim," I said.

"Well, of course he is. He had his own bypass surgery. I'm sure he'll be here soon."

But alone with me, she railed when I told her he was staying home and only visiting every other day.

"I'd be dead without you. I'd have gone into that surgery like a homeless person with no one there for me, if you hadn't come. Was he here the night they operated on me? When was he last here?"

Later she says, "I think your father really believed he needed to take care of himself and get through his own rehab while I was in the hospital so that he could care for me once I came home."

I shake my head at this.

"What? You don't believe that?"

"Mother."

"Well," she says, drawing it out a bit. This is her way of indicating that she thinks I am wrong and that the conversation is over.

I shake my head again and she turns away, sighs heavily. If she could, she'd light up a cigarette, but it has been more than two years since a Marlboro last sat cradled between her lips, probably 20 years since she smoked her most favorite Kools.

My mother knows the truth of my father. Arguing my point would be just another stab to a heart riddled with holes. I imagine my mother's heart like the night sky, except that the stars are a thousand pin pricks of pain. Does she notice them? Are they visible to the human eye? How would the addition of one more star change her galaxy? In actuality, it likely wouldn't change anything. They are stuck, the two of them. Fixed objects, no more able to move away from each other than the moon is able to move from the sun.

HIGH DEFINITION

Before I was out to anybody except my two best friends, calling Judy my "roommate" seemed dangerous—as if people could see the configuration of our bedroom and know that it only held one bed. Additionally, it felt disrespectful. Each time I called her "roommate," my stomach lurched and a part of me flared in anger that I had to deny my true self and the woman I loved. There is something very soul-wearying that occurs when you consistently disavow who you are and who you love and, in those years when I pretended I was just sharing a house with Judy until "one of us gets married," the denial pressed in on me, crowding out other, subtler emotions.

If, as Charlotte Linde writes in her book *Life Stories,* "Narrative is among the most important social resources for creating and maintaining personal identity," then not being able to find the words to tell the story of my life and love left me with a sense of ontological insecurity, the feeling that I was not a wholly integrated person, not capable of coping with the stress of social interaction. In plain English, it meant I felt edgy and isolated from all but those who knew the real details of my relationship. In 1984, it did not even occur to me to appropriate existing words—"straight" language—to describe myself, my love.

⇥ ⇤

I did not want to go to Judy's department Christmas party. All of the rehab staff—doctors, nurses, physical therapists, occupational therapists, speech pathologists, and aides—would be there with their spouses. I would be the token spousal equivalent. Still, our friends Sutton and Lisa (an OT at the hospital with Judy) were hosting and we'd been to their ranch house for drinks and dinner many times. Plus, I had met most of these people at Sweet Tibby Dunbar's, a bar with a great happy hour where you could get a slice of prime rib for free as long as you bought two watered-down drinks. Judy and her co-workers loved to go there on Friday nights—a girls' night out before *Sex and the City* popularized the idea—and, even though I was a "spouse," I was a woman and therefore allowed to attend. Or, maybe it was that I wasn't exactly a "real" spouse.

So, there we were, on the night of the party, standing on Lisa and Sutton's front step. It was raining and I'm sure I wasn't wearing a coat. In those days, I wanted to dress more butch, but I was afraid my clothes would advertise my sexuality, so I wore a haphazard fusion of men's button down shirts, monogrammed sweaters (my mother's attempt to feminize the crew neck I favored), women's peg-legged khaki pants, and androgynous suede bucks. Sort of 1950s preppy and not really very feminine, but somehow better than the 501s, French-cuffed shirts, and Frye boots I secretly wanted.

We opened the door and stepped into the foyer. The party was in full swing: loud conversation and laughter, Christmas carols coming from the stereo, ice jingling in highball glasses full of gin and vodka and bourbon (we all still drank back then and drank hard). The living room was directly across from the entry, and on the far wall was a grey velour couch. One of the older physical therapists— a busybody who seemed to know everyone's business, and if she didn't, made a point to find it out—sat on the couch with her husband. As Judy and I entered, this woman pointed directly at us and turned to speak directly into her husband's ear, finger still aimed at us. Ah, there's the lesbian physical therapist and her "spousal equivalent."

The title seemed amusing at first—spouse in all but name—and it served a purpose because we had no official name for gay and lesbian partners. Spousal equivalent seemed like a good solution because appropriating straight language seemed brash, seemed like we were just asking for trouble. Besides, by this point, we'd come to relish our sub-culture, wanted to live outside the mainstream, or at least not have to follow the strict gender and relationship roles we saw our straight counterparts struggle with. Still, it didn't quite capture the love and commitment we felt, but it was better than roommate, that's for sure.

I'm not exactly sure when I first called Judy my partner. I know I had been thinking of her as that—this must have been in 1992 after we'd officially come out to our families—but I'd not yet said the word out loud. I remember shopping in an art gallery, looking for a painting to give to her for Christmas. The sales clerk hovered. The country was in a recession and I'm sure sales were down. As I walked through the gallery, the clerk peppered me with questions: "What was I looking for? Who were some artists I liked? Watercolor, oils, or silk screen? Originals or prints? Framed or not?" Finally he asked if I was shopping for myself or "someone special." He actually said this, but I suppose he is to be forgiven because this was the early 90s and the beginning of PC language and the tail-end of obsequious yuppie-dom.

"I'm looking for a Christmas gift for my partner." I flushed, I'm sure. If photos from the period are a guide,

I likely had a mullet and wore high tops with baggy, elastic-hemmed weight-lifter pants à la MC Hammer. I could be nothing but a lesbian—especially after uttering the p-word.

For a long time after that, the clerk said nothing, but continued to shadow me at a discrete distance. Finally, he said, "When you said 'partner,' did you mean business partner or partner-partner?"

I realize now that a man working in an art gallery and interested in that distinction was probably gay, but at the time, I felt as if Joseph McCarthy himself were questioning me. The language was new even if the sentiment was not, Ellen wasn't yet on TV, AIDS was just starting to be slowed by AZT, I was still homophobic, and according to Gallup, 51% of the country believed homosexuality was not an acceptable lifestyle.

"Business partner."

"Oh, that's what I thought."

Maybe my memory fails, that it wants more *story* here, but I remember him sounding disappointed, perhaps a bit dejected that he had not found a kindred spirit.

I left the gallery without buying anything.

I finally knew what to call Judy, but it still didn't always feel safe to say so. In 1992, the percentage of people surveyed by Princeton Research and *Newsweek* who reported that they had a friend who was gay or lesbian, worked with someone who was homosexual, or had a gay or lesbian family member was 22%, 20%, and 9%. We were still hidden from the mainstream, represented by the media infrequently (and as deviant when they did cover us), and did not fit outside of the boundaries of the liberal cities and our subculture.

I have a dramatic, 20-something friend who came out recently to one of our mutual friends. My young friend said it didn't go well and she was distraught because, "You only get to come out once."

"No you don't," I said. We were standing in the dappled sunlight of the quad where we both attended graduate school.

"Yes. You. Do." She made a chopping motion with her hand with each word she spoke.

I disagree. Every time I used the word *wife*, I came out, forced recognition. Like the time in 2003 when I was wearing a blue silk suit and leading a group of Indian tech executives through an exercise to help them develop their company story. These men—engineers who had received their degrees from MIT, Cal-Poly, and Harvard—had all returned to India for arranged marriages and then brought their new wives to Silicon Valley where the women started up households and the men started up a tech company.

I stood at the head of the mahogany table in their conference room—the only woman— helping them refine the company's elevator pitch. My sapphire and diamond wedding ring glimmered under the spotlights aimed at the table. I began questioning the three men. "When you introduce yourself," I asked the one closest to me, "what three things do you tell people?"

"That I'm an engineer, that I've been married four years, and that I'm a CTO at a tech company."

We went around the table in this fashion and then I said, "When you introduce your company, what three things do you want to say about it?"

"Wait a minute," one of them said. "What three things do you tell people about yourself?"

It was a fair enough question, but each of them had revealed their marriage as one of the three things they always tell people, and I'd been ducking the question because I wasn't sure how to answer. *Yes, my wife and I have been married 19 years.* Or simply, *I've been married 19 years,* and let the assumption be I was married to a man.

This was in the Valley in 2003 and, by and large, these men had revealed themselves (by their arranged marriages and the fact that they were wearing ties in their own conference room) to be very traditional. "I've been a writer since 1987, I work only with tech companies, and my wife and I have been married for 19 years." And through my use of language, I got to come out for the first time all over again.

⇒⁛ ⁛⇐

That contract was worth $75,000 over the course of a year and this was a calculated risk on my part that could have easily ended with a loss of business—not because these men were necessarily homophobic, but because straight people become uncomfortable when queers appropriate their language. For many Americans, their attitude towards gays and lesbians is: "I don't mind you as long as you don't act gay in public." But, as we have become more visible, more out, and it's easier to look and act openly gay, the crime we are accused of now is appropriating language and institutions (marriage, child-rearing, and the PTA, come to mind).

So calling Judy my wife or, my ex-wife (as is the case now) could be—in the right situation—as incendiary as holding her hand in public would have been 20 years ago (at least, holding her hand outside of the Castro or the Village). The rate of linguistic change has not yet caught up with the cultural change.

This makes sense, according to Mark Pagel whose 2007 study, published in the journal *Nature*, showed that frequently used words (be, have, two, love) evolve more slowly than infrequently used words. Pagel asserts that "the frequency with which specific words are used in everyday language exerts a general and law-like influence on their rates of evolution." I started calling Judy my "wife" before the first gay marriage lawsuit was ever argued in Hawaii in 1996, before DOMA, before the Supreme Court overturned Bowers v. Hardwick. I started calling her my *wife* because I'd worked really hard to come out of the closet and I'd be damned if anyone tried to claim my relationship wasn't just as *real* as anybody else's.

⊷ ⊶

Once every ten years, the Merriam-Webster dictionary is updated. Their 11th edition for 2003 included more than 10,000 new words, along with 100,000 new meanings to existing words and 225,000 revised definitions. The online version, however, posts updates quarterly, and in 2008, it defined the word "wife" as: "a female partner in a marriage."

No mention of husband, no mention of male partner, even though Dictionary.com defines a wife as: "a woman joined in marriage to a man; a woman considered in relation to her husband."

At least according to the editors of Merriam-Webster, the language had evolved.

For years, words were used to oppress. "Faggot," "dyke," "queer," "bulldagger." But then the gay and lesbian community took those words that were originally meant to harm and began wearing them like a badge of honor ("Why, yes, I am a dyke. Thank you for noticing."). Now we are enlightening the world about same-sex relationships by taking on the words "girlfriend," "wife," "boyfriend," "husband"—choosing what we will be called, choosing to celebrate our authentic selves in word, and leaving behind

all the ambiguous words we used to call our lovers—
"roommate," "partner," "significant other," "spousal equivalent," "long-term companion."

What I call my mate matters both to her and the public, although maybe it matters most to my *self* because it
means that I am living openly, I exist. By using girlfriend
or partner or wife, however, I am always prepared for the
conversational pause that can occur the first time—and
sometimes each time—I use the word.

The first time my mother heard me call Judy my "wife,"
she snapped back immediately, indignant and righteous,
"What does she call you? Her husband?"

My voice dropped a notch. "No," I said, drawing out
the "o." "She calls me her wife."

I can't remember what my mother said next. Maybe
she just harrumphed in a bit of linguistic discomfort, maybe she asked why I didn't use the word "partner" instead. It
was as if appropriating straight language was beyond the
pale. Oh, you can be out, you can get married, you can get
divorced, you can date anew, but please, Kate, leave the
language alone.

But, I wanted people to recognize our relationship,
and language was one way to make that happen. I didn't
need the right to marry—although, at this point I hadn't
really considered all the legal protections marriage

afforded—because appropriating straight words seemed to subvert the paradigm almost as much as the rite itself. Maybe even more so because a big butch lesbian saying, "my wife" and "twenty years" in the same sentence forces the listener to think. If gay marriage isn't legal, how can she say this? Does this mean her relationship is no different from mine?

⇥ ⇤

In my life with Judy, I did the bulk of the cooking while she did the laundry and the house cleaning. I mowed the lawn and she kept our houseplants alive. I dealt with the care and cleaning of our vehicles and she weeded our garden. There were no prescribed roles because we did not have to follow social mores. One of us was not the "man" while the other played the "little woman." Everything was open to interpretation and negotiation, and everything was connected to our individual strengths, likes, and dislikes. But once we started naming ourselves, our attitudes—or, at least, mine—shifted ever so subtly. Judy seemed to become more "wife-like," nurturing and tending to the details of our life. I became more "husband-like," earning a big income which allowed her to go to graduate school full-time and begin a new career without significantly affecting our finances.

Looking back, I am chagrined to see that my version of wife had a taint of administrative assistant to it as I relied on Judy to manage the niggling details of life that I disliked. Was it that I believed that's what wives did? Or was that just the dynamic in our relationship? Or did appropriating this straight term cause us to caricaturize our marriage?

Calling Judy my wife loudly and repeatedly reassured me that my relationship was real and asserted to everyone else that it was no different from their own pairings. "Wife" said, "We are just as married as you are and in love." "Wife" meant, "I am committed to you and I will assume the problems in our marriage and work on them." "Wife" was what I married and who I was (even though contrary to what I told my mother, Judy only called me her wife in private; to the public, I was still her "partner," which is what I wanted).

An old friend—a woman I'd not seen in 8 years—was in Portland visiting, and I went to a party given for her, to chat with her and a host of other friends I rarely see.

"Where's Judy?" my friend asked.

"Oh, we divorced this past year."

"I'm so sorry."

"It was really hard but ultimately the best for both of us, I think. If there is any such thing as a truly amicable divorce, this was it."

"But it's not a *real* divorce, right?"

It was a sunny Saturday in August and we were sitting outside under a patio umbrella, sipping Sangria and eating brie cheese on water crackers. A sort of day in which you wouldn't expect the bitter sound of vitriol to creep into your voice.

I took a deep breath. "Well, let's see," I said, "we had to split up two pieces of property and all our investments. We had to visit an accountant, a financial planner, and a title company to remove me from the house. Then we had to split all the personal property in the house, so I'm not sure how that isn't a 'real' divorce. It felt pretty *real* to us."

But I suppose that question is fair, even if it wasn't asked in the most tactful manner. If there is gay marriage, there must be gay divorce. What my friend was really wondering was, "Were you two legally married?" In this case, I suppose, the language caught up the cultural current before I did.

I can talk about my "divorce." But what I have difficulty saying is "ex-wife." I use the term with my therapist and friends, and sometimes even my family, but when talking to people I don't know, I can't seem to get the words out of my mouth. They feel so personal, as if I am outing myself both as a lesbian and as a failure. As if having a lesbian ex-wife gives fuel to the right wing: "See, I told you, Reverend Falwell, those relationships don't last because they are a perversion of god's law." Yet, this is part of recognition, too, that relationships fail for gays and lesbians just as they do for straight people. So, I continually reframe the argument in my head; after all, my marriage did last 23 years. That seems like a success when you realize that according to the US Census Bureau, most first marriages only last 7-8 years and 50% of *all* marriages end in divorce. In light of that, it seems as though Judy and I should be held up as role models.

It took such a long time for our relationship to be recognized as legitimate by our families and society. Judy's family, in particular, believed our relationship was "empty and loveless," and I think they had been expecting its demise all along, as if we didn't have, *couldn't have* what it took to go the distance and make marriage work. So now that Judy is my ex-wife, some small part of me cringes knowing they anticipated this, knowing that the 46% of people who oppose gay marriage anticipate the same result from the thousands of marriages performed legally in California, Connecticut, Delaware, Hawaii, Illinois, Iowa, Maine, Massachusetts, Minnesota, New Hampshire, New Jersey, New Mexico, New York, Oregon, Pennsylvania, Rhode Island, Vermont, Washington, and Wisconsin.

I didn't ever expect to have an ex-wife. Of course, I didn't expect to have a wife, either. At least not one I talked about openly. Wrote about. Introduced as "my wife Judy." The prefix "ex" is from the Latin for "out of, from; to remove from, without." This woman helped make me who I am. I am *from* her. We grew up together. Came out together. Figured out roommate, spousal equivalent, partner, and wife together. And I have *removed myself from* her, as well, expurgating my history as well as my heart.

BRUNCH

Here is the life we said we wanted. Well, actually, it's the life that I said I wanted and you agreed with me. But in hindsight, I wonder if you came along with me simply because you were uncertain of what you wanted and the scene I painted for us didn't seem like a bad one. I said I wanted stacks of *New Yorkers*, strong, good coffee, big, oaky red wine, books, leather furniture. I said I wanted a house with lots of woodwork and good light—a home full of random objets d'art and beautiful, geometric patterned Persian rugs. A life where we could have big dinner parties on Saturday nights and then go out to brunch on Sundays. We could eat at a place like Zell's with big picture windows and an old mahogany soda fountain for a bar.

Everything hinged on brunch.

Here is what brunch offered us: a sense of possibility. If we could eat in a charming café with these big windows; if we could talk and laugh over a basket of scones and cups of bad coffee; if we could talk about what we sought to sow once it warmed up, you sketching out a garden plan with a ballpoint pen on a napkin; if we could talk about your job and my story ideas, then we could go home to our un-renovated Edwardian with the brown shag carpeting and unfinished woodwork. We could return to the pink Formica kitchen table and cheap botanical prints; we could live with the green linoleum in the bedroom and the painted doorknobs; we could go home to all this and know that at some point we could have the life we were dreaming of.

The reality was, well, the reality. After college, we moved to a red suburban house, not the inner city. That was too dangerous, at least that's what they said. I wanted Berkeley and graduate school stimulation, the San Francisco Bay and its beacon of gayness and passion. You wanted order—calm, serenity, rectitude—not artist chaos. I remember desperation. You walking away.

"Can we finish? Help me understand."

Shaking your head—grim, frustrated—you spoke finally. "It's your dream, not mine. Go, if that's what you really want to do. But I can't."

You meant "won't." You would not go, but you thought I would. Another easy ending. Like Eric, Larry, then Mike. Finally, the girl: bye-bye, Katie. But I needed you, thought I'd die. Alone, I thought I was empty and ungrounded. I had no roadmap for leaving, guess I missed that class.

I stood silent. We were falling apart in the garage, of all places. I leaned on the washer, you rested back against the dryer. The blue Toyota Corolla sat in the garage, out front the primroses were bedded down in bark-dust. Inside, the books were shelved alphabetically, beef was roasting in the oven and, on the orange Formica counters, a bottle of red was open, breathing, as two glasses sat waiting. Everything so normal. So normal looking.

Anyway, I failed. Berkeley rejected me. Surely self-sabotage. I had stellar clips and recommendations, but a weak personal statement. I left nevertheless, took a writing job in Seattle, four hours away, but kept my books and desk in Portland. I was an I-5 yo-yo: Seattle, Portland, Seattle. We were never apart enough, never together long enough, to heal our hurt, to push past our own well of loneliness. Yet, still we loved.

And we forgot the discomfort and the drama. Only you existed for me with your turtle eyes: wise, kind, compassionate. And so we began again, crafting our life together in a new house—the dilapidated grey Edwardian with a red Braun coffeemaker on the counter. We left work early, spent afternoons on Sauvie Island eating quiche, drinking Semillon Blanc. What did we know? And still occasional, tentative touching—or more perhaps. Have I forgotten? What about the hour-and-a-half rule? It was so long ago I can't quite remember. In this house, right? Sundays after brunch in the window at Zell's, yeah?

This was back before our neighborhood was gentrified and the only places to have breakfast were Cup & Saucer, the Hawthorne St. Café, or Zell's. It would be another 5 years before the Cadillac opened, another 10 years before Milo's or the Cricket Café. And Wild Abandon didn't offer brunch yet. It was so much edgier back then, the unrenovated houses with their asbestos siding and yards overgrown with rhododendrons untouched by pruners and limb saws in more than 30 years. The random meth house. The Vietnamese gangs. We felt like pioneers pushing our way into the urban wilderness. We felt like adults. Brunch in particular made us feel grown up. So civilized: the fresh-squeezed orange juice, the hash with chutney, the white napkins. In my memory, they're linen and radiant, practically illuminating the silverware set against them. In reality, even in the old days when Tom's mother made the table bouquets of sweet peas, and freesias, and violets, the napkins were paper. Ah, but such was the power of those brunches. Zell's was so good back then, back before everything changed.

STAY TUNED

We got our first Chet Atkins CD along with the JVC tower stereo system that first summer after we'd graduated from college. We played the music loud and opened up the sliding glass door so we could hear it out on the deck where we sat drinking cheap Rosé wine from Chateau Ste. Michelle where Michael got a 40% discount.

We both loved that CD, but you may have loved it even more. You loved the speed of Atkins playing, the dominant sevenths and flatted fifths that gave his music a bluesy slide. We were happy then, I think, even though we were living in the suburbs in a tiny house with no insulation. Life was simple: you got off work at 4:00 p.m. and came home. My barista shift ended at 2:00 p.m. and so I played house, making us quiche and spinach salad, and chilling the Rosé or the Semillion.

I'd be waiting for you, the windows and slider and front door open, Chet Atkins or Rickie Lee Jones or Holly Near on the stereo (we had a single disc changer and were so poor that we only owned three CDs and knew them all by heart). We'd sit on the deck in our blue and white vinyl chaise lounge chairs and watch thunderheads form over the coast range. That summer was the hottest on record and we always hoped for rain to cool things off before we went to bed, but all we ever got was heat lightning.

CAN YOU HEAR ME IN THAT CLOSET YOU'RE IN?

And so you want to talk to her, to tell her, you really do, you have since you were 14, but it isn't any easier at 24, you still have absolutely no idea how to start the conversation, tell your mom that all those insults your dad hurled at you and your friends—Kelly, Linda, Bunny, Gina, Niki—all those insults and innuendos were true, are true, you love girls—dyke, lez, carpet muncher—you like having sex with your own kind, with the one you've been living with for the past five years, that girl you met your first year at college, in the freshman dorm, the girl next door, the only girl you've ever really kissed, that girl—now your roommate—well, yeah, she is literally that (the mate who shares your room), and you just want to tell your mom that you're happy, that you love this girl (although sometimes things seem off and you're not sure if you really want a red house in the suburbs, a house with bark dust and primroses and a lawn that needs mowing every week during the wet Oregon spring, but, who knows, because this is your first real relationship, the first girl you've ever dated, and besides, no one is there to give you advice or tell you that everyone wonders about their life choices, it's perfectly normal and you are right on track).

So yes, you are a lesbian even if your lover isn't sure what she is, but I mean, come on, do you just say that? "Mom, I'm a lesbian." Because, well, don't you think she knows, I mean how could she not, you and your "roommate" have been living together for five years and you wear 501s and men's shirts with French cuffs and didn't go to your senior prom or seriously date any boys—except for Ken Finn, but he doesn't count because he was really in touch with his feminine side and had long hair like a girl—and really, a blind man could see you are a lesbian and so do you even need to say something so entirely obvious? I mean, shouldn't your mom really start the conversation because she's the adult, because she's the one always imploring you to stand up straight, pull your stomach in, drop your shoulders back and would a perm and a little eye makeup really kill you?

But your mom just keeps puffing on her Kools, blowing the smoke up at a steep angle above everyone's heads, but still straight in your direction, unapologetic about her cigarettes even after three hypnosis workshops—the second one for half price, and the third one free, and then finally her money back—she keeps lighting up and asking you questions and talking about everything except your life, like do you think the crown molding she had installed in the family room gives the illusion of height and how this will be the last year she manages the yard without help because the redwood and the eucalyptus need pruning, and the birds of paradise need to be split, and the fruit trees need dormant oil spray, and your father won't help with any of this, and so she will hire it out to McGovern, the man who originally landscaped the yard after the pool went in.

And all the time you are listening to the boom, boom, boom of blood in your ears, and feeling the heat of color in your cheeks, and your fast rabbit breath coming and going in the top half of your lungs, and you are thinking, *Okay, now, say it now.* But how random to blurt out right after the story about pruning the privets, "I'm a lesbian." And besides, lesbian? Or gay? Lesbian seems sort of an ugly word—like vagina or scrotum—so maybe gay, then, because homosexual is so clinical and it's usually preceded by militant and followed by agenda. So forget homosexual, in fact, forget talking at all. At least right now. At least for today.

Begin again with a new tactic—a copy of Randy Shilts' book, *And The Band Played On*, in hardcover with the dust jacket still on. You set the book down on the kitchen table, move towards the counter and begin fixing your coffee—measuring out tablespoons of oily French roast into the one cup filter, filling the kettle with fresh water, turning to the new black side-by-side refrigerator to get the half-and-half, glancing casually to see if your mom has noticed the book and picked it up, read the jacket, your entrance into the conversation, you standing with the little pink and white carton of Clover Brand half-and-half in your right hand, your left thumb hooked casually into your jeans pocket. It's about the AIDS crisis, you'll say. I'm reading it because so many of my friends are HIV-positive and dying. Although this isn't strictly true. But men *are* wasting away, dying in the arms of lovers, and alone, and the obits in cities like LA, San Francisco, and New York are full of oblique mentions of "longtime companions"—so even though your friends aren't dying, you figure this is a credible, newsworthy way to raise the gay topic and segue into your own story about gayness. That's the word you decided on: "gay."

Except that your mother seems not to have even looked at the book sitting right there on the table, all 630 pages of it buzzing off and on like a neon sign just advertising your gayness, your lesbianosity. Your mother lights a second cigarette, match tip to tobacco, blows the smoke away from the book, the cloud traveling toward the hutch full of your grandmother's and great-grandmother's china and sterling flatware, and the delicate crystal wineglasses your mother registered for before she married your dad, and unlike the thick, pedestrian glasses you bought for yourself at Cost Plus. And so, you say nothing about the book, the men, your life with women—say nothing because your mom hasn't noticed the book and besides that quarter-sawn oak hutch with eight cupboards full of family history presses on you, the oldest daughter and first grandchild, as surely as if an earthquake had toppled it onto you, which, if you tell your mom about your sexuality before breakfast, just may happen.

And then when it is done, you are relieved and nauseated at the same time. A hush falls over your busy mind covering the rough edges of worry and anger like snow on a field of wheat stubble, and you wait in the quiet to see what will happen next.

If you could have done anything else, you would have. But you are a six on the Kinsey scale. For one time in your life you wish you were not such an overachiever, a little more average, a three, say, and you probably could be a happy bisexual like one of your younger sisters. AC/DC your mom calls it. But instead you are on the highway to hell. You came out with a six, the mark of the beast, although your parents aren't religious. They didn't ruffle your hair looking for 666. Maybe they didn't need to. Maybe the cap gun in the holster that you insisted on swaggering around in when you were four years old was enough. Or at eight when you wanted to go to school in the brown suede saddle shoes and hip hugger jeans slung low across your tiny pelvis. Or the 501s and black watch plaid flannel shirt you did wear to junior high when you were 14. Or the tuxedo you wore in a few shots for your high school senior portrait. You suppose your parents didn't need Alfred Kinsey to tell them you were a six.

Maybe finally coming out means that you can act like yourself when you go home. Maybe you and your partner can stop spending holidays apart like single people who go home to their respective families and wish their "friend" long-distance glad tidings and okay-talk-to-you-laters, instead of opening presents together on Christmas morning, hair uncombed, still in pajama pants and t-shirt tops, drinking cups of dark French roast and listening to the Nat King Cole Christmas CD and that mixed CD with the Beach Boys version of "I'll Be Home For Christmas" that the two of you got when you bought your Calphalon pots and pans together at Williams-Sonoma. That song always makes you cry because you haven't been home for Christmas, at least not home with the woman you love. Except maybe this year you will be home, together.

Maybe it will all be different now that you have forced a recognition. Maybe you can sit together at your parents' house, in the living room, on the floral couch, your parents in the white velvet chairs flanking either end of the couch. You can sit with your hand on your girl's thigh, sip a gin and tonic and have general happy hour conversation, although you're not quite sure what that is—small talk, perhaps—except that would be weird in your own family. So scratch that.

Instead you are at the mahogany dining room table. A silver well-and-tree platter with a perfectly browned turkey atop it sitting at your father's place and he carving the bird tableside. Your sisters and your mom laughing and confiding in your partner, "Oh, when Katie was little she loved . . ." The clink of Waterford crystal as you all toast Happy Thanksgiving or Merry Christmas. You know, something different from what it's usually been: your father sullen and angry; your mother late to the table because she's been crying in the back bathroom; your sister with Asperger's Syndrome staring at her plate and not making eye contact as she eats her way through white potatoes, sweet potatoes with marshmallows on top, stuffing, and dinner rolls (*Nope. Not eating turkey. Tastes like you just licked a metal railing.* You've called her Rainman for years and the Asperger's diagnosis, when it comes ten years later, doesn't surprise you or your other sister, although your parents will never quite believe it); your other sister glaring at you because you yelled at your father for making your mother cry (*Jesus, Kate, why do you hate Dad so much.* It's as if her memory has been erased). And now your partner is here, too, looking calm, but actually working very hard to seem innocuous, look inconspicuous, and use her powers of Vulcan Mind Meld to calm the whole situation or, at least not get drawn into the fray.

You come to recognize it as a compliment—that your family acts no differently once you are finally out and visiting with the woman you call your wife more regularly. They shout and stamp their feet. They pound off dramatically to their separate rooms. They say egregious things. In short, they act like they always have and they expect you to do the same. And so you don't rest your hand on your wife's thigh during happy hour or hold it under the table during dinner, squeezing it to reassure her, because even though you've finally come out, your parents have said don't act gay in front of us, by which they mean just act like the good friends you always pretended to be. Well, okay, it was your dad who actually said this. Your mother said she was glad that you didn't have "one of those lesbian haircuts," which you assume to mean a mullet, all short in the front and long in the back, and for crying out loud, being a lesbian does not automatically mean you have no fashion sense, play softball, and eat organic tofu braised in hemp seed oil. Still, it is a relief to finally be able to breathe fresh air for the first time in 14 years and not the stale air of the closet you've been hiding in. The hardest part is over, you think. The rest is just clean-up.

WHAT I WON'T WEAR

MAC or Bobbi Brown. Maybelline and Cover Girl are out, too. (Although, Estee Lauder and L'Oreal make excellent moisturizers and everyone needs well-hydrated skin. And sometimes, I'll wear a little Aveda brand lipstick just to freak my girlfriend out and because, in a strange way, it's almost gender bending.)

Mini-, midi-, or maxi-skirts. A-line-, drop-waisted-, jumper-, or sun-dresses. A shirtwaist, a sheath, or a shift. A cocktail dress or a ball gown. A Kitty Foyle or a St. John's Knit. A tunic. A crinoline. A bustle. That said, I don't mind wrapping a Sarong around my waist (and over my shorts) to visit Catholic cathedrals in Latin countries. It's sort of my butch version of a skort. Although, it's not exactly flattering.

A twinset, cap-sleeved t-shirts, or anything called a blouse. A chemise, a spaghetti-strap tank top, or a tube top. A smock or a turtleneck (Because I'm not a painter and my neck's too short). A shirt with a Peter Pan collar. A choli or anything where my midriff hangs out.

Nylons, thigh-high or otherwise. Of course, Spanx are a miracle of modern technology that our forebears fought for—a 21st century alternative to the Merry Widow—and which I believe have their place in the well-dressed butch's wardrobe.

Court shoes or elevator shoes. Platforms, stilettos, or kitten heels. No to mules and pumps, too. No to Manolo Blahnik, Jimmy Choo, Charles Jourdan, Christian Louboutin, and Bruno Magli. (Unless you're talking about his two-tone oxford or the big-buckled chunky heeled loafer. But you're not, are you? You mean his wedges and his spectator pumps, don't you? In which case, no means no.)

STRING OF PEARLS

I am in Nordstrom at the end of the summer doing a little back-to-school shopping. My mother looks at dresses for me. But I am in the men's department fingering silk t-shirts and the beautiful French blue, teal, and purple cotton shirts with button-down collars. I don't feel so good about myself, partially because I gained 25 pounds instead of the usual Freshman 10. My clothes feel much too tight and I spend most of my days wearing oversized shirts untucked so that I can leave the first one or two buttons of my jeans undone. But shopping for new clothes means this: me looking at men's shirts and tailored pants while my mother looks at satiny shirts with shoulder pads to make me look "slim," and skirts, and dresses that are "sharp" or "smart."

It is almost better, I think, to wear jeans two sizes too small than the blue, paisley dress my mother showed me before I disappeared from the women's section altogether. And we were in the "women's" section—Encore, Nordstrom calls it—as in, "Call the tailor: we need an encore to cover this one." Women's clothes make me uncomfortable as a rule, and *women's* clothes—as in fat women's clothes—not only make me feel uncomfortable physically and psychically, but make me feel unfashionable, as well. As if the only things a fat girl should be allowed to wear are polyester pants—preferably "slimming" black—and floral polyester tops or cotton camp shirts in an Easter egg palette.

And dear God, I look awful in all these clothes, like I just escaped from some Amish or Mennonite mental hospital, which is why I am downstairs lingering by the men's shirts. I *fit* into a men's XL. A few of these shirts and some of the new pre-washed 501s in blue, black, and white (after all, it is 1984), and I would be set for the school year. But I know better than to ask. These are clothes I will have to buy for myself on some other visit.

So I am standing here alone feeling fat and unattractive and when I look up from the dress shirt with the button-down collar and French cuffs, I see an elegant femme with long strawberry blonde hair. She is wearing a tight, wool, navy-blue skirt with a kick pleat, a cream-colored blouse (silk, I'm sure), and a choker of pearls. She is tall and the blue spectator pumps she is wearing make her even more so. On her arm is the butchest woman I have ever seen. She is equally tall and wearing expensive clothes: wool gabardine trousers, riding boots (their black sheen poking out from under the cuff of her pants), and a perfectly pressed man's shirt. As they walk by me, the butch reaches over and pats the femme right on her beautifully rounded backside and follows its line which is so apparent against the tight wool. My jaw drops. I have not yet seen lesbians of this ilk: college-educated, wealthy; nor have I yet seen such an openly gay public display of affection. This femme looks back over her left shoulder, sees all this on my face, and lets go a delicious peal of laughter. I start after them, but like an apparition, they have disappeared into the store.

WHAT I WILL WEAR

I t's fraught for all sorts of reasons.

Because when I came out it was not politically correct to be butch or femme—buying into the dominant paradigm of gender expectations and all that. Because I have been socialized as a woman even as I have railed against the Maybelline, and MAC and all those ridiculous outfits that require you to sit—with your thighs demurely pressed together. Because—and it pains me most to admit this one—I care what you think. I want you to like me and not judge me simply because I favor patterned ties in a double Windsor knot.

It's easy to dress for everyday. There's no issue with slim-fit, colored chinos—especially if they have a button fly. Burnt umber, cobalt, sage green, fire truck red, and aubergine, all hang in my closet. A hard finish so the pants wear well is preferable, but brushed twill is all right, too. Everyone is wearing these now. Even Costco sells Gloria Vanderbilt colored jeans for women. And if I wear mine rolled at the hem like a J Crew male model or a Kennedy summering at Hyannis Port you likely won't even notice.

Special events are more, shall we say, challenging. Do I wear the black, summer-weight wool, pinstriped pants, custom-made for my 5'4" frame? Blue or black twill pants, the de rigeur look of business casual? Plain front or pleated? I'm starting to cross that gender line—now you're going to notice.

Crew neck t-shirts, I favor these. Long sleeve is, more often than not, better than short. (Somehow it's more formal and completes my favored high-brow/low-brow look—jeans, a t-shirt, and an expensive vest or blazer.) Of course, I also like hip shirts cut from Italian cotton, and made by Bugatchi Uomo, Duchamp, or Robert Graham. Something with subtle checks, reversed out cuffs and collars, and square buttons, something that when paired with my perpetually flushed Irish cheeks and soft face gives me a gender-bending look. I'm afraid you'll notice my transgression, but I also love to transgress. See, I told you it's *fraught*.

But now the tie, bow and otherwise. Patterned more often than not. This is the big one. A tie is like a giant fucking billboard that says, "Ask me about my gender identification!" Here's the rationalization that I make each time I'm standing in the mirror, collar up, tying under, over, behind, and through: a patterned tie is ornamental, and loose at the neck, charming, less chance of people thinking you're just an angry dyke trying to make a point. And please don't call me that unless you are. A dyke, I mean. Straight people—even liberal ones—don't get to use that word.

The shoes. Ropers and cowboy boots can work. Frye boots if it's a hipster event—same thing with biker toe black oxfords. For meeting clients or dinners out, suede wingtips or saddle shoes with outrageously garish laces are stylish and whimsical. Wingtips made with shiny Cordovan leather dyed tobacco brown or midnight black are too much. Too much what, I'm not entirely sure. Too butch—yes. Too gender non-conforming when paired with the rest of my ensemble—sure. Too much of an in-your-face statement—maybe. Even though these shoes feel right on me, I don't think I have the ego strength to carry off wearing them.

Finally, the foundation. Boxers or briefs? Sports or push-up bra? Wouldn't you like to know.

QUITE SUDDENLY. ALL AT ONCE. FINALLY. AT LAST.

You are both lying there not sleeping and breathing much too fast. And maybe you are whispering to each other, your heads close together. Maybe your foreheads are touching. Or maybe not. At any rate, you surely are whispering because your parents' bedroom is right on the other side of yours. You can hear your father snoring. You can also hear the TV in the family room and you know your mother is still awake, smoking and watching Johnny Carson. You are whispering because you don't want to get caught awake, thinking the thoughts you are thinking.

Then, you don't know how it happens, but suddenly the sides of your mouths are touching. Maybe you both turned toward each other too quickly. It's hard to say. But, at any rate, you are kissing. Quite suddenly. All at once. Finally. At last.

You whisper to the girl to crawl on top of you, the better to kiss her hard and not crush her thin bird bones. She grinds her nylon underwear against your cotton ones. You slide a finger under the leg elastic, but she pushes your hand away and says "no." You feel her coarse, straight pubic hair, so different from your own before she puts you in your place. Without warning, though, she pulls off her shirt. You take yours off, too, and then there is that delicious moment when her fabulous, fecund breasts first touch yours. It stops your breath. Nipple to nipple. Roundness to roundness. It is a scene you will both like to play over and over in the years to come.

She says, "How do you know what you're doing?"

You want to say, *Duh! I was born to do this.* Instead you say, *I don't know.*

She asks again.

You answer the same way, and also add, *I just do.* You sort of shrug, but she is on top of you, so it's hard to do.

She whispers urgently, "Have you done this before?"

You tell her the truth: *No.*

You try again to get underneath her thick, woven nylon underwear. No lingerie, these. They feel like a bathing suit that been snagged against the rough plaster of a public pool. Or a Speedo that's been covered in salt water and left to dry in the sun. But once inside, you can feel she's interested.

"Don't," she says.

It's okay, you say. And this time she doesn't stop you.

You continue this way all night long. Finally around 4:00 a.m. she falls asleep. At 5:00 you rise and slip from the bed, take your car and drive all over your suddenly-very-small town looking for someone—anyone—to tell your secret to. Your heart is singing, but your head is in a vice grip, the pressure of non-conformity threatening to crush your skull.

There is no one to tell. You are alone in your deviance.

Before anyone else in your family awakens, you come home and slip back into bed. But she is awake and worried.

"Where were you?" she asks. Her voice sounds young and panicky.

Driving around, you say. You are crying a little.

"I was afraid you were going to tell me I had to go home and I was trying to figure out what I was going to say to my parents when I showed up."

I was afraid you were going to wake up and hate me for making you gay.

She pulls you to her and you finally sleep. When you wake near noon, only the two of you are home. And so you begin again for the first time.

LETTER TO A YOUNG BUTCH

I have a picture of you, two of them actually, when you are 16 years old. In the first photo, you are with Niki, Pip, and Suzie. You are touring with a group of musicians and singers, performing gigs across the US and Canada. The oldest in the group is only 22 (you call him a semi-professional authority figure), but somehow your parents still let you go even though they must, *must,* have the lack of real adult supervision, which is why you are posing for this photo, on your way across the country in one of two converted school buses painted with flat, white house paint, and full of duffle bags, instruments, sound equipment, food, kitchen utensils, and Niki, Pip, and Suzie. Three young gay kids and one who would grow up to be a homophobe.

You are wearing 501s, white Nikes, and a white baseball jersey with red stripes on the arms that you bought at the Army surplus store. You got the shirt specifically to wear on tour, knowing your mother would never allow you to attend school dressed that way. The shirt is made from heavy cotton jersey, too thick, really, to wear on a bus with no air conditioning rolling through the Midwest in June. But you like the way you feel in this shirt and your Levis. It is like these clothes somehow fit you differently than the scoop neck shirts with lace appliqué and corduroy pants or the cowl-necked sweaters and poplin pants that your mother buys you and wants you to wear during the school year. Your jeans and t-shirts and the white Nikes—classic now, with the turquoise blue stripe—are a pleasure to pull on each morning when you wake up, starting a new day in a different city, on your way to another small town for another show. You like being on your own, getting dressed and eating breakfast without your family, not having to suffer through the accusation of your mother's thinly pressed lips, lips that seem to say, *you're wearing that?* Your mother doesn't need to say anything; you know how she feels about how you look. On tour, you don't have to swallow down a lump of maple-flavored buckwheat flakes, summon strength you aren't sure you have and look her in the eye defiantly, even as your cheeks blush with shame, and say, "Yes. I am wearing this." Instead, this morning, the morning the picture was taken by both Jill Johnson and Lynn Pritchett—you have copies from each of them—you rolled out of your sleeping bag, pulled on your clothes and sighed into yourself, at ease, for once, with who you were and how you looked.

I can see it in your body language, the way your right arm drapes casually over the back of the bus seat and rests lightly on Niki's shoulder. Looking at this picture from a distance of 30 years, I can see the chivalry in your gesture, although you wouldn't have known to call it this. You are more worried about not touching Niki too suggestively, no caress of her plush girl arm, your breath steady, your eyes forward.

Or maybe you are not worrying about this. You are laughing and so is she, her mouth open wide, her white teeth dazzling. Twenty-seven years after this photo was taken you will have lunch with Niki and introduce her to your new girlfriend who will wonder aloud why you and Niki were not girlfriends. "It just didn't turn out that way," you'll reply. The truth is, you were too full of internalized homophobia to even consider making a move. But looking at this photo today, the sparks are visible even at this re-move. Did you wish Suzie wasn't there, sticking her blonde head into the photo, so you could pull Niki just a bit closer to you? Probably not. Then, it was just enough to have your arm lightly around a girl's shoulder.

Pip is in the background holding a curling iron and striking a pose like Jose Eber, hairdresser to the stars. He is wearing a flamboyantly huge silver belt buckle and Ray Bans—aviator style—a precursor to the Dolce & Gabbana sunglasses I suspect he now favors. You, Niki, Pip: I imagine you're all feeling an inkling of your sexual destiny. Well, more than an inkling, but you're quiet about it. It's more a gnawing in your gut, a sense that things aren't quite right. It is only late at night, after a few beers, when you are alone, that you allow yourselves fleeting thoughts of sex with another, sex with the same.

Looking at this photo, I know what awaits all of you. It's visible in Pip's curling iron camp, the way Niki leans toward you, your nonchalant body language, a young butch already enthralled with the divine feminine. And yet, I also see three young gay kids—babies, practically—happy and laughing, unaware of the therapy and anti-depressants coming their way. Niki will fall in love with a girl named Reggie but end up with a man named Pete. She will be pregnant with his child—a Christmas party lapse in judgment—and will marry Pete because she believes her son needs an intact family. She should know this, bounced as she was between her father and mother, not exactly wanted in either home, ultimately living on her own before her 17th birthday. During your freshman year at the University of Puget Sound, you will fall in love with a woman and recognize it for what it is. You will miss the first opportunity to kiss her as you are standing on the Marin headlands watching the sun set over the Pacific, the shining beacon of San Francisco at your backs. Later that night, you will not miss your cue and you will continue with her for more than 20 years, through undergraduate and graduate degrees, through seven different houses and three different couches, through deaths and catastrophic illnesses, for better or worse even though you are not legally permitted to say those words.

It is Pip whose story you'll never really know. He will graduate from Sacramento State and move to San Francisco to begin a career in advertising. Each time you see one of your old friends you will ask, "Is Pip gay yet?" When you finally hear news that he has come out of the closet, you will rejoice for him. The oldest son of an Ecuadoran patriarch, you imagine the agony Pip must have felt embracing his sexuality against that culture and tradition.

In the next photo, you are again with Niki. You stand between her and another woman, your arms draped around both their shoulders. This time you are wearing a button-down Oxford cloth shirt and a fedora that is tipped slightly forward. Your chin is angled down and towards Niki, your eyes twinkle mischievously, and a slightly smug smile creeps across your face, as if to say, *Yes, in fact, I am looking good for the ladies.* It is rare in pictures taken during these years to see you look so self-assured. Usually you are clowning in front of the camera or are caught still, unaware that the lens is trained on you and so a slight longing around the edges of your dark Irish eyes is visible. Or at least that is what I see in you all these years later.

Niki also looks happy and maybe a bit cocky. She is flashing her bright white teeth and the camera catches her as she is chomping on a piece of gum, just visible on the right side of her mouth. She is wearing overalls and her "The Moose Is Loose" baseball jersey. You all wore them that year—I think it was 1982—providing free advertising for Moosehead Lager, a beer you had never tasted.

In these two photos, who you are—and who you are to become—is evident even though you can't yet feel it. And so I want you to listen. After the bus stops and you are alone in your blue sleeping bag—lying on a gymnasium floor in Elko, Nevada, or on top of a pool table in some youth center in Niagara, New York, lying there thinking about a girl or the life that is coming instead of sleeping—listen hard and maybe you'll hear the vague echo of your future self and the voices of all the women waiting for you: Judy, Peg, Kris, Lucy, Lauren, Biz, Dorothy, Mary, Catherine, Kate, Barbara, Elisabeth, Candice, Julie, Frances, Katrina, and, of course, Niki, along with all the other unnamed women who will help you walk tall into your destiny. Listen for them and do not give up hope. But also relish times like those captured in these pictures, where you are in the moment, happy to simply have a girl—or even two—on your arm.

CURE

Jess Price ran to his grandmother's waiting car every day after school. He only lived one block from San Ramon Elementary, but his grandmother received special dispensation from the principal to pick him up in the parking lot. The other mothers idled their station wagons up and down San Ramon Way, chatting or not, smoking menthol cigarettes or not, and waiting for their charges. But everyday, rain or shine, Jess Price's grandmother's Cadillac waited in the parking lot only steps from the school.

Stephanie Caldwell, Dawn O'Connor, Nancy Adams, and I. We walked the four blocks home. Even in the rain. Unless you lived more than a half mile away you were supposed to walk. Except for Jess.

Nancy Adams got the idea to beat him up. She told us to hide behind the pillars supporting the school roof and, when Jess ran his personal gauntlet from classroom to Cadillac, we'd jump from behind the columns one after another, like doing the wave at Candlestick Park. We'd each smack Jess, getting off one good punch before he ran on; hit him along his well-defined jaw or on his prominent nose. Maybe a thrust right to the orbit of one of his blue eyes.

I lay in wait behind the last column, my back pressed against the cool concrete and listened for the sound of Jess' low-top Converse slapping the pavement. His gait was uneven as first Nancy, then Dawn, then Stephanie jumped from their hiding places.

My turn. Bam! A smack right to his head, my fist crashing into his blonde temple, and then Jess' grandmother screaming, "Come on, Bubke! Run!"

"Faggot!" I shouted. The word felt foreign in my mouth. Wrong. Dangerous. Powerful. "Faggot," I shouted at him so no one would shout "dyke" at me.

We sensed Jess' fear and his weakness, the way you catch a scent of honeysuckle wafting up on a warm day or smell a lingering bit of perfume after a beautiful woman leaves a room. We smelled this and turned on Jess that year, like a pack of dogs descending on its weakest member, leaving him to circle the fringes and lap up whatever shred of kindness might remain.

Two years later: who knows what happened to Jess Price. The story was that his grandparents transferred him to Hill Junior High, the school for the blue-collar kids, where they thought he'd be safer. Away from the entitled, elitist white kids who tried to smear out different-ness with a punch, a designer label, their parents' European cars.

The Hill kids scared us. They didn't care how they were dressed or in what type of car their parents drove them to school. Because if their parents didn't drive them, it meant they were still drunk from the night before or stuck working a crap shift stocking shelves at the Safeway, mopping floors at the community hospital, changing bed pans at the nursing home. When you're worried that you might come home and find your mom drunk or you haven't gotten enough to eat—and this being Northern California circa 1977, there are no free lunch programs or even a cafeteria, just a snack bar selling Hostess Twinkies, Reser's burritos, and corn dogs—well, if you're worried about survival, you probably don't care very much about an effeminate Jewish boy who lives with his grandparents and has no other after-school activity except reading ahead in the text book.

The rest of us went to Sinaloa Junior High. The summer of love had ended, but our proximity to San Francisco meant that we could still buy loose joints for a buck in the locker room next to Mr. Roberts' classroom. Mr. Roberts in his overalls and big, black Frye boots looking, I realize now, like a classic Castro man. He rode a Honda Goldwing to work which explained the boots, I suppose. But there wasn't much that could explain the red bandana poking out of his right back pocket or the big black leather wallet connected to the heavy silver chain. Or the earring. The shaved head. The goatee. Roberts stood over six feet in his boots and the overalls covered a significant gut. No one called him faggot in—or out—of the classroom. Sometimes the older kids mentioned the Castro and leather men, but these words sounded as foreign to us as fellatio, rimming, and handballing.

I loved Mr. Roberts' geography class. But more so I loved to see the spark of recognition in his eyes. I believed he realized how smart I was and sensed what I felt was my certain bohemian charm. Clearly, Mr. Roberts saw how misunderstood I was.

Yes, clearly.

I try to imagine what it would be like to have a child as I was. I came in butch—of this I am sure—and yet, I was blonde and pink cheeked and very obviously a girl—a girl craving pants, t-shirts without pink satin bows, and a holster and cap guns, which my mother confiscated when I was three. She didn't have any moral opposition to playing with guns. It's just that her two-and-a-half foot tall daughter in the yellow stirrup pants wanted to swagger everywhere with that holster on. There were rules: you can dress yourself, but only wear pants three times a week. The holster, of course, was out of the question.

So when, at age 9, I dreamed of pressing my body up against Coleen M, the youth leader of the Catholic church, I began lying. I loved the boy next door, the boy down the street, the boy in the next city. There were rules: I could say I liked boys but only ones with the same initials as Coleen—Chris Mellon, Charlie Maddox (a boy I reprised in college, in order to throw my parents off my lying, lesbian trail).

And at 12, when a brutal leg cramp required my swim coach to help me from the pool, I could not bear to think about what my coach's hands felt like as they encircled my chest and she pulled me to the far end of the lane. There were rules: swim 100 laps in 30 minutes and I could allow myself to imagine Jean rescuing me, my hands in place of her hands. If I stopped to rest after 50 laps, I could think about my rescue but not touch myself.

At 14, there is Barb N, my eighth grade English teacher at Sinaloa Junior High. There are no rules now. I cannot believe how this woman makes me feel. She rubs my shoulder and my body betrays me. She tells me she loves me, that it isn't sexual, that women can love other women in a nonsexual way. Yeah, maybe in your world, I think.

My crush is written all over my fair, Irish cheeks which blush each time I gush about Barb. My parents are beside themselves, fearing I'm being molested into the "homosexual lifestyle." They needn't have worried, though. This woman was doing a fine job of mind-fucking me, making me believe I could sublimate my sexual energy and live straight.

"Write it all down," she says, her finger at the back of my neck. "You're a gifted writer."

Later, I hand her a month's worth of writing, chronicling my growing awareness that my sexuality is inevitable, inescapable. She reads it all and hands it back with only one comment, "Are you trying to convince yourself or me?

She asks me to have lunch with her. I'd been standing on the corner of the campus where Wilson Road met McClay. Standing by myself and brooding when she pulls up in her brown Fiat Spider, the top down, and motions for me to get in. We drive off together, the heat on, the smell of ocean and eucalyptus permeating the foggy Northern California air.

"I'm taking you to my house." She reaches over and takes my left hand in her right.

I've tried for years to find that house again. It's off McClay Road, back in the hills. It's vintage Northern California, a house all windows and skylights, a glassed in porch, two stories of redwood shake. You entered on the ground floor and climbed an oak stair case, past white wainscoting, up into a chaotic kitchen with butcher block counters and copper pots and a stack of unwashed breakfast dishes sitting on the drain board. A picnic table covered in an oilskin and the *New York Times* was pushed up against a wall of windows that looked onto the second story porch, sheltered by more windows and the boughs of big oak trees. A colander of fruit sat on the butcher block island, along with a stack of mail, and, perhaps, more dishes. The whole place redolent with the scent of cinnamon and coffee. There may have been undertones of ripening fruit and sexuality, but after 28 years, I cannot be certain what I remember, what I intuited, and what I've imagined.

We'd driven to the beach together a few months earlier. But that is not exactly true. She had driven me to the beach. I was not yet even eligible for my learner's permit. On the way to Pt. Reyes, we stopped at the cheese factory and I remember buying us cheese and bread and dark chocolate, a young butch beginning her own seduction of femme women. Yet, I cannot have had the money for this and I cannot believe that Barb would have let it go that far. Still, I know we sat letting the quiet and wild wash over us and ate cheese and bread that someone purchased.

I wore 501 jeans, a white t-shirt, and a blue plaid flannel shirt. I know because the only reason this day happened was that my mother was gone, back in Minneapolis visiting her own mother. There were rules: no Levis at school, no contact outside of school with that woman.

But in the kitchen of her house where she'd taken me this time, I was wearing green dittos—with the famous horseshoe seam meant to flatter your backside—and not 501s and so I'd lost my young butch swagger. I sat quietly, looking at the table top while she busied herself fixing us lunch. If she seduced me—and oh, god, I wanted her to—everything would change. If she would only kiss me, release in me the terrible yearning that gnawed in my gut, the awful ache in my groin. Just a kiss to confirm that she felt it, too, that I wasn't alone in my feelings, in my desire for another woman.

Instead, we sat at the picnic kitchen table and ate sandwiches—tuna, I think—that were too dry and caught in my throat. I remember us not talking, the sound of the bread as it squeaked between my teeth and stuck to the roof of my mouth, the hum of the old Frigidaire with the big metal pull-down handle, the strange ringing in my ears a harmony to the thud, thud, thudding of my heart. I don't remember anything else. Not the drive back to school, not getting out of the car at the corner of Wilson and McClay roads, as I surely must have done so that Barb could drive up to the campus alone.

I do know that I didn't kiss her. It would be five years before I got another chance to really kiss a girl.

Heather N screams at me in the driveway of her mother's house. "Why don't you get your own fucking mother? Why the hell do you always have to sneak around here?"

She's right. I walk by Heather's mother's house every day to see if her car is in the driveway. I have lunch with Heather's mother. I drive to the beach with Heather's mother and I want to spend the night with her on the big waterbed in her living room. I want to do unspeakable things with Heather's mother. The same mother who is, perhaps, not there for Heather. Heather, who does not see her father since her mother left him, does not want some 14-year-old interloper taking away her mother, as well. Heather's mother who rubs my back and brushes her lips across the top of my head and the back of my neck. Heather's mother who understands the terrible knowledge coming to me and yet who doesn't see what befalls her own daughter. Heather's mother who betrays her by failing to notice her daughter's hunger. Heather's mother who betrays us both.

"Why don't you get your own fucking mother?"

I have no idea how to respond. I turn to leave, say nothing that betrays the fear I feel at being outed.

I sat on the white velvet chairs in my parents' living room. The sky rested like a lead weight on the green Northern California hills that rose around our town. On top of the Baldwin piano sat two 8x10 photographs. One showed my mother in profile, wearing a wedding gown and smiling beatifically. The other was of my Aunt Ginny, the woman who married my mother's brother. This is what parents wanted for their daughters. This is what normal women wanted.

Except for me. Which is why I'd come to the living room with a Henckels chef's knife and was scraping the blade across my left wrist. I could feel its sharpness and knew if I pulled it down my wrist, the knife would easily open the vein right below the skin's surface.

For the first time in months, my head felt silent. The voice that called me sick and lez, that told me I was a disappointment to my parents and would live an abject, lonely life, said nothing. Everything settled to the bottom of my brain like silt.

I thought the knife would cure me. Or if not cure me, end my suffering. But I couldn't do it. I didn't want to wreck the chairs. They were my mother's favorite. And so I sat there and waited, wondering how soon until my parents knew I was a lesbian and disowned me or sent me to some re-education camp in Utah.

Yet I cannot have known about Utah, known about reparative therapy. But I knew this story about a man my mother had cared for in 1959 while working as a student nurse at the University of Minnesota. His name was John and he came to the University for an experimental treatment—electro-shock therapy—that showed promise of curing homosexuality.

Every day, John received a jolt of electricity to try to fry the gayness out of him. These were the early days of shock therapy and the wattage the doctors ran through John in 1959 was much, much more than they use today. Unsedated, John was shocked three times a day Monday through Saturday and twice on Sundays, his body contorting in agony, unearthly cries escaping the carefully sequestered room and drifting up the hallway. I imagine the smell of singed hair wafting up along with those cries.

What happens when you wake from that procedure and find you still prefer your male doctor to your female nurse? How many times do you put yourself through that? In John's case, more times than had ever before been documented. So many times that the university ordered "treatment" discontinued before John was "cured."

I wish I could say that I knew about Jess Price, tracked him down and learned why he lived with his grandparents, what happened to him. No one I went to school with knew about him—or even remembered him until I reminded them. Was Jess gay? Did he contract HIV? He and I became sexually active in San Francisco around 1981, right when the first cases of the mysterious "gay cancer" had just started metastasizing throughout our community. And yet, the city still shone brightly then, a beacon calling home all the dispossessed, the disenfranchised, the different. Maybe Jess also stood on the periphery of this bright shining gayness, afraid to act, afraid of what it would do to his relationship with his family, afraid of what it would mean to himself.

I'd like to think that I'd recognize Jess if I saw him on the street or in some gay bar in the Castro, but I can't be sure. I imagine he'd look like any ageing 40-something gay man: hair cropped close to minimize the effects of male pattern baldness, biceps pumped big to assuage lingering doubts about manhood or sexual stamina, clothes a mixture of funky chic and expensive brand name.

I hope that Jess would be striding down the street, his head held high, unafraid and sure of his place in the world. Maybe a man would walk next to him, his arm sloping down to Jess' hip. Or, maybe he'd walk alone and the sun would catch the gold of his wedding ring, slid onto his finger by a man who loved him as they stood on the steps of San Francisco city hall in February, 2004. Maybe on Valentine's Day or George Washington's birthday. The irony of marrying a same-sex partner on the birthday of one of America's founding fathers would not escape the still-bookish Jess.

If I saw Jess, I don't think I'd speak. Instead, I'd just lean against the door jamb of the Twin Peaks bar, the first gay bar in San Francisco with windows facing the street— windows that let passersby see the bar's patrons, men sitting with other men unafraid—and I'd watch Jess slide by.

MURMURATION OF STARLINGS

I am too young to know much about relationships, or the ingrained belief which almost all of us carry that we are lucky to have what we've gotten thus far. I am also too young to know much about fear and how it both paralyzes you and makes you rabid, leaving you snarling and vicious, and chained in place. That's why it is not until I am 16 years old that I ponder the unthinkable: why doesn't she leave him? Does she simply not see how he is, or does she deliberately not want to see?

What I can't know is that years later, when I am 43, I will go to lunch with my parents. They will be driving through town on their way to California. It will be May and warm, and we will sit outside at a brewpub, waiting for our hamburgers.

Apparently, my father will have recently shot a starling.

"Had to." He will sit, hands crossed and resting on the table. He will look almost earnest, like he's being interviewed for a job. Except—by this time— my father will not have worked in almost 20 years.

"Tell her why." My mother will sound disgusted, afraid to keep all to herself the knowledge of his darkness. She will egg on the story. "Tell her."

"I don't need to hear this," I will say.

"It was the other starling's spouse. It kept sitting by the nest, waiting for the other bird." He will laugh as he says this.

"And your father had already killed the other bird."

I will nod, signal the waiter for another pint of beer.

"I just put this one out of its misery. Quick shot to the head and he dropped," he will whistle and make a corkscrew motion with his finger. "Had to. Couldn't bear to see it sitting there or should I say, shitting there." My dad will laugh again, pleased with his pun.

I will shake my head.

"Do you see what he's like?" my mother will ask.

THE PATRON SAINT OF
LOST CAUSES

Today is some saint's day, some holy day of obligation and my father feels—I think—some strange mix of obligation and longing for spiritual connection. This manifests on the surface as Catholic guilt. Ford Mustangs, Grand Torinos, and Mercury Marquis wagons jam the church parking lot. So different from my mother's Episcopal church where we attend regular services, and park our Volvo station wagon next to Mercedes, BMWs, and Saabs. Our Lady of Loretto Catholic Church is for alternate high, holy holidays and obligation days. But today, we are either too late or my father forgot that it is a saint's day. He slows as we pass the church on the corner of Grant Avenue and Novato Boulevard, and glances over at the entrance, stucco with an overhang to keep post-service congregants out of the Northern California winter rain. Mary looms above the far right corner of the architectural protuberance, her femininity and breasts hidden within the folds of fabric that drape every representation of her, her sexuality as mute and concealed as my own.

The church doors stand wide open, four sets across, to funnel in the Irish, the Italian, the Mexican, and the displaced Midwest Poles, but the conspicuous lack of people means chanting, incense, and prayer already fill the church.

My dad grimaces slightly, continues to focus on the straight two-lane ribbon of Novato Boulevard.

"I always said that when I made enough money I'd build a church to honor St. Jude." My father breaks my reverie by speaking.

"What? Why?"

"Because he got me out of some bad situations."

I am only 16 and don't have the language to ask what I want to ask and, besides, I am scared of the answer he'll give me. In my family, we don't ask the hard questions and perhaps because of my father's military training and my mother's WASP heritage, we also don't offer up any unsolicited information. Don't ask. Don't tell.

I'm not sure what I thought then about the "bad situations" St. Jude delivered my father from, but the image that comes to mind is this: my father crouched low, pinned down in the humid dank of some Southeast Asian jungle in the years before the Bay of Pigs or the Gulf of Tonkin resolution. Snakes and not so small rodents work their way through the detritus of the forest floor. Birds screech and cry. A twig snaps. The diphthongs and tones of Cambodian, Laotian, or Vietnamese pierce the air as surely as gunfire. My father's heart boom, boom, booming in his ears. Capture seems imminent and I imagine my father offering up a prayer to St. Jude: "It you get me out of here, I will build a church to honor you."

But he's not told me this story. He continues, "St. Jude is the patron saint of lost causes."

My father's religiosity does not shock me. He and I have attended church together many times. What surprises me about what my father just told me is the seriousness of his tone and the idea that he prayed for deliverance outside of the 50 minute confines of a church service.

⤝ ⤞

Each morning after this conversation, I read the "Personal" want ads column of the *San Francisco Chronicle*. There, in column inches and black-and-white, are prayers and thanks to St. Jude: "St. Jude, thank you for the safe return." Or "St. Jude, I beseech you to reveal lost object." The ads—paid for by the word—rarely list what has been lost—and so I imagine freely: a runaway child, a grandmother's diamond ring, virginity, faith, an errant husband.

When I read through those pleas, I always look closely to see if I can recognize a message from my father among the entreaties. By the time I open the paper, he's already left for work, though, and so I never lift my head, look over the top of the newsprint and say, "Dad, listen to this one. What do you think it means?" Or, "Dad, maybe you should place an ad and just save that church money."

EXCEPTIONS

Here is what I remember: My father sailed on the USS Burton Island and the USS Coral Sea. The former took him to Antarctica and the latter to Southeast Asia, the jumping off point for covert operations he conducted for the Office of Naval Intelligence. But that comes later. Or earlier, as it were.

The way my mother tells it—or told it—at least, the way I think she told it, and I never asked my father about this, so I only have my own memory of a third-party telling to go on here, was that when my father finally resigned from the Navy in order to marry my mother, he and my mother and some of their friends sat at the Cliff House in San Francisco, high above the Pacific, and watched as the Coral Sea left Treasure Island without my father, to steam its way across the Pacific, next stop Hawaii, then on to Asia. The power was out at the Cliff House—a rolling brownout overheating the grid—and the champagne was warm. Still, the party toasted bon voyage and good riddance to a system hell-bent on destroying a generation of men. Except now my mother says this wasn't true, isn't true. That my father was never on the USS Coral Sea. Even the champagne is suspect now.

My father's commanding officer was a man name JW LeDoux. Whether he was a commander then or merely a lieutenant commander doesn't matter, I suppose. LeDoux was my father's senior and the officer in charge of his fate. According to my mom, LeDoux refused to allow my father to resign his commission.

"You know what that little man said?" she asked recently.

I can recite the answer, but it's not required.

"He said, 'Forget about her.'"

As she ages, this is the only part of the story she will hang onto. That some man thought my mother should be left behind. She will tell me I've made up the entire story about the Cliff House and the Coral Sea. Besides, she will say, and I'll see her focus go soft as she remembers the Cliff House and its view, how could you even see all the way out into the shipping lanes?

⊷ ⊶

My mother used to tell what I think of as the whole story. She said that my parents first met LeDoux at the Officers' Club on Treasure Island. My father wanted to introduce his fiancé to his CO. He considered LeDoux a father-figure, I suppose. Later, according to my mother, LeDoux asked my father why he wanted to throw away a naval career on something as transient as love. Then he said, in reference to my mother, "She's a lovely girl, forget about her."

My father refused to acquiesce. I imagine some sort of negotiations ensued. The story I think I know is that my father ultimately threatened LeDoux with a *New York Times* expose of the US covert operations. Shortly thereafter, he received an honorable discharge on January 15, 1964. Which leads us to the Cliff House, the warm champagne, and the USS Coral Sea sailing towards Southeast Asia with all her screws turning.

Except my parents were married three days later in Minneapolis and couldn't have been in the bar at the Cliff House because my mother had been in the Midwest since Christmas. Except, a little digging turns up two pictures of the USS Ranger, an aircraft carrier also deployed to Southeast Asia. And that bastion of knowledge Wikipedia says, "She set sail again for Eastern waters out of San Francisco on 2 February, 1962, patrolling in the South China Sea as crises and strife mounted in both Laos and South Vietnam." His redacted service orders show him only on the USS Burton Island and the USS Klondike. But there are these two pictures, tucked into a letter he sent to his parents, saved all these years by them and then him. "Parents, Mary and I thought you'd like these photos. Your son, John."

Except when I am 49 and tell my mom about this, she says my dad wasn't on the Ranger. "I had friends on the Ranger," she tells me. "I would know if your father was on the Ranger. He wasn't."

I will never once ask my father about his service. I somehow understand it would be a dangerous thing to do. No questions about counter-insurgency training. No questions about where he served. I will only have fragments of conversations. *When you're flying in below the radar, it's a bumpy ride. I favor a .45 for a sidearm. You know how many poisonous snakes there are in Vietnam? That's where they decommission ships – right over there – it's called Mare Island.* And I swear, *That's the USS Coral Sea there. Your dad was on that.* Except that the USS Coral Sea will not be decommissioned until 1990, in Norfolk, Virginia. When I am 25.

The Klondike was my father's cover, I think. A repair ship that sailed between San Diego and Subic Bay in the Philippines. My father trained for covert operations on one of the archipelago's 7,000 islands, but I will only discover this a few days before his death.

"Are you afraid to die?" I will ask him. His back, ribs, and femur will be constantly at risk of shattering as the metastases from his esophageal cancer tat away at the bones.

"No. What's scary is sitting in a black metal box with a python crawling over you."

This will be the first time he ever mentions a non-humorous story about his naval service. I will learn from my mother that he'd walked across China and Laos, and I assume Vietnam. When I am in grade school, he tells me about being in Manila, and the wharf rats the size of cats who were able to jump the cones on the ship's lines and work their way onto the deck. I will not want to blow the moment at his bedside by asking too much.

"In the Navy?

"In the Philippines. Training for black ops." His eyes will unfocus, the light grey irises clouded by macular degeneration and narcotics.

"What did you do?"

"Sat very still."

I will want to ask more, but he'll say quietly, "I don't want to talk about this anymore."

Once he's dead and my mother's memory failing, she will insist that my father didn't sail on the USS Coral Sea or have his aviator wings. The latter despite the gold wings in his officer's jewelry box and his membership in the Association of Naval Aviators.

"Oh, they let anyone in that group," she'll say when I ask. "You just had to be in the Navy."

This will turn out to be true, and make me doubt myself even further and hang onto my mother's patchy memory. But even as I doubt the USS Coral Sea, I will hold fast to the belief he flew planes and I will obsess with finding a picture of him in dress blues with his wings above his service bars. There are few pictures like this and, in the ones I find, his left shoulder is angled away from the camera lens, the service bars – and possibly his wings – hidden from view.

I don't know why this point will become so important to me except that there will be no one left to tell me what the truth is – or rather, what the facts were. Maybe this is the greatest lesson I will learn from my father: the truth is one thing, the facts are another. Most of my life, I will believe they are the same thing – synonyms – truth and fact.

But the facts are that the naval orders show that my father was a Lieutenant Junior Grade in the United States Naval Reserve from December, 1960 to January, 1964. The facts show that he was dispatched to the USS Burton Island and the USS Klondike before ultimately being approved for discharge by JW LeDoux in order to marry my mother which, in truth, he should have never done.

WEATHER REPORTS

Growing up, I watched my father's moves like a meteorologist watches the sky tracking cloud formations moving slow and dark across the clear blue, trying to predict the collision of hot and cold air and the storms that might ensue. Or whether said clouds would unexpectedly turn north and dissipate. It was more art than science though, and my predictions often fell flat: thunderstorms on the third of July, the fourth with its alcohol and shrieking children and fireworks remaining clear. Other times, the barometer fell without warning and my sisters and I would scarcely have time to drop the canvas shades over the porch screens before wind and lightning and rain began all at once.

Sometimes I'd wake to the sound of my father's voice, low and menacing, like a long rumble of thunder. My mother's voice hissed like rain on a hot sidewalk and it was difficult to hear what either of them had to say without leaving the safety of my bed. I'd lie there, listening to the thunder and praying to Jesus and my dead relatives that there would be no lightning, that the power wouldn't go out, that I wouldn't have to press myself against the long wall of the hallway and make my way to the cane rack and slowly withdraw one of the sticks.

Sometimes the storms came late enough at night that we'd sleep through them. We'd wake the next morning to a world that seemed right but subtly different. Maybe a little extra humidity in the air or my mother's lips set in grim determination against the elements. It was clear something had passed through, but now was gone.

LEARNING TO WALTZ

I try to imagine them in their first year together. I say *try* because for all the stories they both tell, they never talk much about this year. Somehow, they secured an apartment in Bloomington, Minnesota, in a blond brick 8-unit building set back from the road by a wide, sloping lawn. My father began working in the tech industry, programming for Control Data. Maybe it was here that he learned the COBOL and FORTRAN. Maybe he sat in his grey flannel pants and white button down shirt and typed into a dummy terminal, the green cursor on the screen winking on and off through the haze of smoke from his Pall Malls. I imagine him 22 years younger than I am now, but already grey at the temples, the grey all the more striking set against the black stems of his horn rim glasses—squinting at the screen while his bratwurst-sized fingers peck out code that is translated onto punch cards that run mainframe computers the size of their tiny apartment.

My mother went to work as an ICU nurse at Abbott Northwestern, the same hospital in which I will be born 13 months later. Look at her: four evenings a week on the ICU floor, moving constantly from bypass to osteotomy—suctioning drains, changing dressings, aspirating patients. Then, look at her back in the tiny one-bedroom apartment, furnished with a pre-existing couch and coffee table. This night, she's home, using Peg Bracken's, *I Hate to Cook* to fix "Lamb Shanks Tra La" for dinner. The book sits on the Formica countertop—white with gold sparkles—and next to a blue-green glass ashtray where a Kool menthol cigarette burns down.

Lamb shanks ensconced in the oven, she and my dad sit down for happy hour cocktails of cheap scotch and water.

"Not that cheap," my mom's voice echoes in my head. "We never drank Four Roses. We weren't that poor."

When do you suppose they first thought they weren't right for each other? My mother tells me she was devastated by their fights that first year, that she confided to her friend that she thought they would divorce, her friend saying that every couple fought. My mother says she thought that she just didn't understand what marriage looked like because her father had died when she was only six or seven years old.

I know the pyrotechnics of the battles they fought when I was a teenager. Alcohol fueled my father and a decade of mostly repressed rage lit up my mother. If their early fights approximated this, I'm sure they both thought a trip to Reno for a quickie divorce was in their future.

I can see my father in the morning after one of these first fights, hair uncombed and wispy, standing on end like a Kewpie doll's. At 27, he already looks jowly and the way he pushes his lips together when he is thinking—unflattering, like a wind-up monkey—exacerbates the jowls, making him look at once like a Bürgermeister and a little boy. In his left hand is a coffee cup with brown and blue stripes; in his right, a Pall Mall, the end hanging with an impressive amount of ash. I imagine my father wanting to apologize to my mother except that he has no idea how to do this, how to say the words. Twenty years later, I will know his apologies to sound like backhanded blame. Forty years later, after the end of my own marriage, I understand that this is partly because he also wants his own feelings—however wrongheaded—acknowledged. But on this morning, in the tiny kitchen of my parents' first apartment, I imagine all my father feels is remorse and fear that he and my mother won't be able to recover that delicious, drugged closeness the newly in love feel.

Look at her: my mother works evenings, 3 to 11, so this morning she is in a yellow nightie, her hair set in the brush rollers she will use nightly for 40 years, until a rotator cuff injury makes it impossible to set her hair. Her back is to him as she works at the stove, scrambling eggs for herself, frying them for him. Her coffee cup—the mate to his— sits on the counter, the last sip grown cold. Her left hand holds a Kool cigarette. She does not want to face him, to have him see her pain and insecurity. Five or 10 years from now, she'll cover those emotions with an icy veneer of anger. But today, all you can see is her broken heart.

He puts his big paw on her shoulder. She moves away, ostensibly to pour short glasses of orange juice, and he returns his hand to his side. In six minutes, over eggs and toast, and second cups of coffee, they'll face each other and begin again, scarcely a word spoken about the night before, and I will watch them continue this dance for 45 of their 46 years together, mimicking the steps until they become my own.

NOTES

The statistics quoted in the essay "High Definition" come from a variety of sources, among them:

Brewer, Paul. *Value War: Public Opinion and the Politics of Gay Rights*. Maryland: Rowman & Littlefield, 2008.

Fields, Rose M. Kreider and Jason M. *Number, Timing, and Duration of Marriages and Divorces: Fall 1996*. Washington, DC: US Census Bureau, 2002.

Gallup Research. May 1992.

Linde, Charlotte. *Life Stories*. New York: Oxford University Press, 1993.

Pagel, Mark. "Frequency of Word-Use Predicts Rates of Lexical Evolution Throughout Indo- European History." *Nature* (2007): 717-720.

Washington Post-ABC News Poll. 2009 April.

ACKNOWLEDGEMENTS

Several essays originally appeared in the following places:

"And So You Begin Again for the First Time" appeared in *Fourth Genre* 14:2

"Boogie Nights" appeared in *Gertrude,* Volume 17

"Can You Hear Me In That Closet You're In" appeared in a different form in *Fourth Genre* 14:2

"Cure" appeared in the *Press 53 Open Awards Anthology 2009*

"Don We Now Our Gay Apparel" appeared in *Pank Online*

"Letter to a Young Butch" appeared in *Southern California Review,* 2012 Volume V

"Sir Ma'am Sir" appeared in a substantially different form
as "Victoria's Real Secret" in *Gertrude*, Spring 2007
"String of Pearls" appeared in *New Plains Review,* Fall 2010
"The Boy Scout Motto" appeared in *New Plains Review,*
Spring 2010
"What I Won't Wear," and "What I Will Wear" appeared in
Fourth Genre 16:1

Writing a collection of essays—like raising a child—takes a
village, and many people helped raise this collection. And
this particular baby would not have survived without the guid-
ance, help, and babysitting provided by my particular village.

Ann Hursey, Judith Pulman, Cindy Stewart-Rinier, and
Christine Robbins: you women took me under your protec-
tive wings when I was broken and barren, and you tolerated
my often futile attempts at writing again. I've learned so much
about rhythm, lyricism, and life from you. Whose house are
we meeting at next? I'll bring the gluten-free pastry.

Erin Hollowell, Linda Martin, Jill McCabe Johnson, and
Eva Saulitis: you'll never know how grateful I was for that
dinner invitation in Boston. And Erin, for all the support
and patience, and for helping me realize I owned my own
creativity.

To my mentors: Sherry Simpson, Dinah Lenney, and Judith
Kitchen. You have always been so very generous with your

time and insights. Judith, in particular, always believed in this work—so much so that she graciously asked to publish it.

Peggy Shumaker and Joe Usibelli: thank you for your big Alaskan friendship, greasy dumplings, and the keys to the condo. And thank you for your introduction to Robert Usibelli, who took the amazing photo on the front cover.

Sandra Swinburne: there are not enough words of gratitude for your gracious offer to step in and copy edit, talk to me about fleurons and margins and the relative merits of centered titles versus left-aligned titles. Thank you also for your friendship, your kindness, and for letting me ramble on about various publication fears. I swear to god I never got your text messages that time you were in Portland!

Theresa Bakker Smith and Heather Weber: I returned to your original comments again and again in the shaping of this manuscript. Thank you for years of insight and friendship.

Daemond Arrindell, Dennis Caswell, Larry Crist, Josephine Ensign, Jay McAleer, Peter Munro, Corry Venema-Weiss, Chelsea Werner-Jatzke, and the irrepressible, irresistible Stevie Kallos: I give you Jack Straw love, gratitude for sharing your journey with me, and holiday cheeseball.

Lesbiana Profundis and Special K: thank you for the beach house where some of this was written, emergency sushi, early morning phone calls, AA support, Bridge

Watch 2012, bike rides, pancakes, and 15 other things I'm probably forgetting.

Thanks to Zan Gibbs for her steady butch hands and DIY ethic. Here's to Z-scores forever.

To the Tines: thank you for your fierce belief in this writing and in me, and for your hard honesty (*I don't know why you aren't dropping everything to work on this*). I promise to make sure there is—from this day forward—toilet paper in every bathroom. And to fix the cabinet door. And to mostly answer the phone when you call. And. And. And.

A very special thanks to Barbara Hort, whose nudging, cajoling, encouragement, and faith sustained me during the years when this manuscript was merely an itch at the back of my brain. For last minutes reads and edits, for cheerleading, for cat videos, and for the reminder that everything dies at last and too soon so you better go out and save your own life. Yes, in fact, you are absolutely and always right.

Finally, to Judy, who lived this story with me for more than two decades. Thank you, Sap, for figuring out with me who we were—and who we were meant to become.

ABOUT THE AUTHOR

Kate Carroll de Gutes is a wry observer and writer who started her career as a journalist and then got excited by new journalism which became creative nonfiction and is now called essay (personal, lyric, and otherwise). Kate holds an MFA in creative writing from the Rainier Writing Workshop at Pacific Lutheran University and lives in Portland, Oregon where she rides bikes, eats gluten free pastry, and can be seen occasionally wearing a whimsical, patterned tie. You can learn more about Kate, and listen to interviews as well as a musical interpretation of one of her essays at www.katecarrolldegutes.com.

OVENBIRD

Judith Kitchen's Ovenbird Books promotes innovative, imaginative, experimental works of creative nonfiction.

Ovenbird Books
The Circus Train by Judith Kitchen

Judith Kitchen Select:
The Last Good Obsession by Sandra Swinburne
Dear Boy: An Epistolary Memoir by Heather Weber
The Slow Farm by Tarn Wilson
The Book of Knowledge and Wonder by Steven Harvey
Objects in Mirror Are Closer Than They Appear by Kate Carroll de Gutes

www:ovenbirdbooks.com

Made in the USA
Columbia, SC
15 January 2018